LET'S GET FREE

LET'S GET FREE

A HIP-HOP THEORY OF JUSTICE

Paul Butler

THE NEW PRESS

NEW YORK
LONDON

Published in the United States by The New Press, New York, 2009
Distributed by Perseus Distribution

LIBRARY OF CONGRESS CATALOGING-IN-PUBLICATION DATA

Butler, Paul Delano, 1961–
Let's get free : a hip-hop theory of justice / Paul Butler.
p.   cm.
Includes bibliographical references.
ISBN 978-1-59558-329-1 (hc. : alk. paper)
1. Criminal justice, Administration of—United States.
2. African Americans–Legal status, laws, etc.   3. African American public
prosecutors—Washington (D.C.)—Biography.   I. Title.
KF9223.B88 2009
345.73'05–dc22   2008053427

The New Press was established in 1990 as a not-for-profit alternative to the large, com-
mercial publishing houses currently dominating the book publishing industry. The
New Press operates in the public interest rather than for private gain, and is committed
to publishing, in innovative ways, works of educational, cultural, and community value
that are often deemed insufficiently profitable.

www.thenewpress.com

Composition by dix!
This book was set in Electra

Printed in the United States of America

2   4   6   8   10   9   7   5   3   1

To my mother,
Lindi Butler-Walton

CONTENTS

ACKNOWLEDGMENTS

The Open Society Institute helped make this book possible when it awarded me a Soros Justice Fellowship. I am grateful to OSI for nourishing my project with both its resources and its fostering of a dynamic community of activists and writers. George Washington University Law School provided indispensable research grants, and the African American Policy Forum gave me both inspiration and cash money, baby.

Much respect to the friends and colleagues who commented on draft chapters. Their insight made this book better. I thank Rachel Barkow, Derrick Bell, Donald Braman, Devon Carbado, Kimberlé Crenshaw, Angela Jordan Davis, Roger Fairfax, Luke Harris, Fred Lawrence, Marc Mauer, Tracey Meares, Richard Pierce, Ellen Podgor, Renée Raymond, Dorothy Roberts, William Rubenstein, Katheryn Russell-Brown, David Sklansky, Christopher Slogobin, Dan Solove, Michael Starr, Carol Steiker, and Deborah Tuerkheimer.

Mad props to the peeps who generously shared their ideas, experiences, and creativity, including Chandra Bhatnagar, Anthony Farley, Jacob Goldfield, Lori Green, Cheryl Harris, Lenese Herbert, Cynthia Lee, Eric Lotke, Sunita Patel, Roger Schechter, Mark Srere, David Zlotnick, and the participants in the 2008 Criminal Justice Roundtable at Harvard Law School and the 2008 Social Justice Writers Retreat.

Big up to the crew whose expertise in, or encouragement of, the book-writing process was crucial: Joseph Beckford, Bernard Bell, Christopher Bracey, Sheryll Cashin, Adam Culbreath, Shawn Frazier, Jacqueline Hackett, Helen Elaine Lee, Jonell Nash, Spencer Overton, Myron Smith, and my parents, Lindi Butler-Walton and Paul Butler Senior. The New Press has been incredibly enthusiastic and supportive, especially Diane Wachtell, Priyanka Jacob, and Ellen Adler.

Shout out to Glynis Hammond, my secretary, and my research assistants Bill DuFour, Jessica Inmon, Adrienne Lawrence, Nima Mohebbi, Ashley Rankin, Juan Rafols, Ezra Sternstein, and Ravn Whitington.

It takes a posse to write a book. I owe everything to mine, which includes family, friends, and my wonderful students and colleagues at George Washington University. Thanks, guys.

The title *Let's Get Free* was inspired by, and is also the title of, the hip-hop artists Dead Prez's debut album (Loud Records, 2000).

The Hunter Gets Captured by the Game: A Prosecutor Meets American Criminal Justice

I am prosecuting a prostitute. She barely speaks English. We are in a room more like a cell than a courtroom. It's in the corridor of the District of Columbia Superior Court devoted to "nonjury," the venue for trials of minor crimes. When lawmakers don't want people to have jury trials for certain offenses, they make the sentence for the crime less than six months in jail; then, according to the U.S. Supreme Court, the defendant is only entitled to a bench trial.

Judges, you see, are more likely to convict than juries. In this hallway, justice is processed with extreme efficiency—a good judge and prosecutor, working as a team, can get through four or five trials a day.

Crowded inside the little room are the prostitute, a court-appointed defense attorney, a police officer, the judge, me, and my mother. It is my mom's first time seeing me in trial and I want to impress her.

The facts of solicitation for prostitution cases are always the same: plainclothes male officer encounters prostitute, she offers sexual favor in exchange for cash, and he arrests her. These are not your high-class call girls but rather streetwalkers—the old-fashioned, skanky kind, complete with pimp, drug habit, and tragic backstory.

It's actually difficult to get arrested for prostitution in the District of Columbia, where it's a crime but not a big police priority.

Everybody—sex workers, customers, and cops—knows what's where: Fourteenth Street is biological women, Ninth Street is transvestites, Fifth Street, not far from the courthouse, is male hustlers. On Friday and Saturday nights there are so many johns and other gawkers they create a minor traffic jam.

Generally nobody cares. It's a business district anyway; at night the lawyers and lobbyists are home in the suburbs, so now it's the streets rather than the offices that are devoted to service for hire. Sure, the police department has a vice squad, but how much can it do, really? The relationship between beat cops and habitual criminals is polite and semirespectful. Each understands that the other has a job to do.

Sometimes, however, citizens complain, especially when they see the cops and the girls yukking it up. Then a showy crackdown happens for a few days. This is just an annoyance to all the principals. The world's oldest profession certainly is not surrendering; if anything, it will temporarily switch corners. Police sweeps don't eradicate crimes like prostitution and drug selling; they just make those activities less orderly.

Most of the girls know who the undercover cops (UCs) are, but my defendant has broken two rules. The police report says that she approached the plainclothes officer and offered to perform oral sex (she probably didn't use those words) for $25. Rule number one: always recognize the UCs.

Second, she has the temerity to actually go to trial, when rule number two is: plead your case. Throw yourself on the mercy of the judge; unless you have an exceptionally long string of convictions, you most likely will get sentenced to probation and a drug treatment program, and you can be back on the street that same night.

You plead because there is basically no defense in these cases other than general denial. And who is a judge going to believe, an officer of the Metropolitan Police Department or a Vietnamese girl who happened to be on Fourteenth Street at two o'clock in the morning in hot pants, a bikini top, and stilettos? Please. And my mother is watching me? I cannot wait for my cross-examination. I am going to let this whore have it.

I am now prosecuting a United States senator. After practicing on the District of Columbia's hookers, addicts, and assorted street thugs, I have graduated to the Department of Justice's Public Integrity Section. Three years into it, I am assigned the biggest case of my career.

Senator David Durenberger, Republican of Minnesota, has rigged an illegal scheme to get the government to pay his mortgage. By the time the FBI catches him, he has defrauded the taxpayers out of a few thousand dollars. After three years of prosecuting public corruption cases, I'm not surprised that some big-time politicians are sleazes. The startling thing is how low their price is.

We have charged the senator with multiple felonies. It's one of the most important prosecutions in the Justice Department. As a young lawyer, I'm lucky to be on the case; I am sure it didn't hurt that I am black. We indicted Durenberger in the District of Columbia, where the jurors are mainly African American.

I'm only the second chair; the senior lawyer, a white guy, is just a few years older than I am but has a lot more experience. As long as I get to do a nice opening or closing statement, and a couple of juicy cross-examinations, I will be a happy camper. This is the kind of high-profile case that can make a lawyer's career. Life, for this young prosecutor, is sweet.

Shortly before the Durenberger case is due to go to trial, I get arrested.

Simple assault is the crime I am accused of committing.[1]

"There is nothing simple about simple assault." That was the joke made, a few years before my arrest—as I was trained how to prosecute that crime—by the Misdemeanor Section Chief, who later directed my own prosecution. What I did not know then—what a man who makes his living putting people in prison cannot afford to believe—is that there is nothing simple about any accusation of crime. I had to learn that the hard way.

"Criminal justice" is what happens after a complicated series of events has gone bad. It is the end result of failure—the failure of a group of people that sometimes includes, but is never limited to, the accused person.

What I am not saying: prison should be abolished; people should not be held accountable for their actions. I don't believe that. I have locked up thugs I hope never see the light of day. I will never deny that society needs an official way to punish the bad guys; otherwise, if somebody did the unthinkable—say, killed my loved one—I would kill him myself. The criminal justice system gives the state a monopoly on exercising that kind of retribution. It's legal hate.

The problem with hate is that it's hard to contain. In the United States the rush to punish is out of control. In addition to the violent creeps I put away, I sent hundreds of other people to prison who should not be there. Their incarceration only makes things worse—for them and especially for us on the outside. We would all be better off if I had lost those cases. We would be safer and more free.

But I was too good a prosecutor to lose much. And then I got locked up myself. So all I am saying is that the shit's complex.

At the beginning of my trial—the trial in which I am cast in the lead role and someone else plays the prosecutor—the judge tells the jury, "This case arises from a dispute between two people about a parking space." Dramatic pause. "Neither one of them drives a car."

The newly sworn-in jurors have put on their serious faces, but a couple of them look amused. I would think it was kind of funny, too, if it was happening to somebody else. I'd joke about it at happy hour after a long day in court.

•   •   •

First, a quick biography, emphasizing the items that make arrest at age thirty-three unlikely: Yale College and Harvard Law School. Both cum laude. Prestigious clerkship with a federal judge. Cushy job at high-powered Washington, DC, law firm. Then, federal prosecutor in the most elite unit in the Department of Justice.

Now the counterstory, emphasizing the items that make lack of arrest by age thirty-three surprising: Raised by single mom in poor black neighborhood on the South Side of Chicago. When not at work, dress, in the current fashion, like a thug. Nice-sized chip on shoulder, afflicted with the black man's thing for respect by any means necessary. Don't like the police much, even though I work with them every day. Can be a smart-ass.

When I left the law firm to go to the Justice Department, I took a substantial pay cut. I had to downgrade my lifestyle, which included moving to a less expensive apartment. I found a great place in a sketchy neighborhood not far from downtown. Included in the rent was a parking space that I didn't need.

I rode my bike everywhere I needed to go. The checkout clerks at the Safeway got a kick out of me coming into the store every night after work. A black man in a suit and tie stood out in this neighborhood anyway. I just added to the spectacle by jumping on my bike, tying my grocery bags to the handlebars, and riding off.

I was happy not to own a car, because parking issues in my new neighborhood were notorious. Leaving your vehicle on the street overnight risked a smashed window and a stolen radio. And that was only if you were lucky enough to find a legal spot in the first place.

So my bright idea was to rent out my parking space. It would guarantee a little extra money coming in every month. I noticed, however, that there was often a car parked in my assigned space. I figured it was just someone who noticed it was never used and had taken advantage of the opportunity. One evening I made a point of catching up with the guy who parked there. "It's my space," I told him politely. "I know it's been vacant for a while, but it's going to be used from now on."

"Well," he said, "I rent it from the lady who lives there." He pointed to the apartment inhabited by a woman called "Detroit."

In the future I would think of her as Crazy Lady, or the Neighbor from Hell, but actually, Detroit is just as descriptive. In one of several bizarre moments during her cross-examination, my defense attorney asked Detroit how she came to be named after the Motor City. She said, with pride, "The government gave me that name." The jury, which by this point had discerned that this was going to be a funny trial, cracked up.

Ironically, that was one of the few things she said during her testimony that was probably true. Barbara Waters was a snitch, or "confidential informant" in law enforcement parlance, and Detroit was probably the code name the cops gave her for protection. However, because Ms. Waters was also a police groupie, she couldn't keep her secret identity to herself. Thus everyone in the neighborhood knew her as Detroit.

She looked to be in her late thirties. She stood about five feet three inches and weighed maybe two hundred pounds. She lived with her elderly uncle and two large German shepherds, whom she referred to as "K-9s." It was not a terrible neighborhood, but it was also not the most hospitable one for a heavyset black woman who walked around trying to look tough. Almost every time Detroit stepped out of her apartment she took her dogs with her.

I met her when I first moved to the complex. The backs of our apartments faced each other across the parking lot. We introduced ourselves and exchanged pleasantries. That was the extent of our acquaintanceship until this guy told me she was renting out my parking space.

Detroit didn't drive either, but I guess we both had a bit of hustler in us: we recognized an opportunity for entrepreneurship when we saw one. The difference was that she had no legal right to the lot. Squatter's rights really don't count for much outside of the Old West.

I knocked on Detroit's door and told her politely but firmly that I needed my space. She replied it was her space. In my best lawyer voice, I announced that I had a document to show her, and produced my lease with space number nine clearly marked as belonging to my apartment. She slammed the door in my face.

Not to be deterred by some crazy lady with delusions of parking grandeur, I rented out space nine to Donna, a twenty-something social worker who walked through the neighborhood with a jaunt intended to communicate "I'm a baaad white girl so don't fuck with me." She had responded to my flyer advertising the parking space the first day I'd put it up, and had been thrilled to find a safe place for her car.

Right away Detroit started accosting Donna, claiming that she couldn't park there. I showed Donna my lease and she said she could deal with Detroit. But then someone started leaving notes on Donna's car that warned of harm to both Donna and the vehicle if she continued to use the parking space.

Making threats, I knew from my day job, is a crime. We both suspected who the culprit was, but we didn't have any proof. If there were evidence, we knew we could get the police involved. So I started to look out my back window, waiting to catch Detroit putting one of the notes on the car. I kept my camera next to me. Maybe I got a little obsessed with it. I am, after all, a prosecutor.

During this time the wood floors of my apartment were being refinished, creating bags and bags of sawdust. On a Tuesday night the workmen left the bags at my building's garbage pickup spot, which happened to be on the street right in front of Detroit's apartment.

I manned my post at the window, watching on and off most of the evening, but didn't catch anyone leaving a note. I woke up early the next morning and, as had become my practice, looked out the window.

There was sawdust all over Donna's car. I was pissed. Throwing on jeans and a T-shirt, I ran outside. No one was in the lot, but right in front of her apartment stood Detroit. Guarded as ever by her two "K-9s," she was sweeping something from her porch. Something that looked like sawdust. I yelled, "I'm calling the police." I might have added "bitch."

First I went over to Donna's car to inspect it for damage. I remembered from my prosecutor training that DC police take claims of destruction to cars more seriously than other kinds of minor crimes. The joke among prosecutors was if your boyfriend beats you up, don't say "He hit me and I'm bleeding" when you call 911. The police will take hours to come. Say "Somebody put sugar in my gas tank" and they'll be there in three minutes.

Donna's car didn't look seriously damaged; there was just sawdust all over it. I headed back inside to call the police when all of a sudden there was no longer a need to do so. Three police cars, sirens blaring, flew into the parking lot. Several cops jumped out, yelling at me, "Put your hands in the air, motherfucker! Lean against the car!" Then came the words that I'd spent my whole life trying to avoid: "You're under arrest."

"What? Why?" I was in a state of disbelief. This had to be a joke.

"Simple assault."

Detroit had called 911 and said that somebody spread sawdust on her porch. She claimed that, as she was sweeping it up, I ran up to her and pushed her and she fell down. She was now suffering from back pain.

That's ridiculous, I told the police. They should call Donna to get the history of the whole dispute. Anyway, who would go anywhere near Detroit with those two big German shepherds standing guard?

The police weren't listening. My arresting officer was a muscular bald man who looked like a Nazi, if the Nazis had accepted applications from Puerto Ricans. So I played my trump card: "I am a prosecutor." The cop looked interested. I hoped this would be an opening. I needed one badly. I couldn't get arrested. I did not go to Harvard Law School to end up just another nigga with a record.

I showed the officer my Justice Department ID. He inspected it carefully. Then he smirked and said, "So I'm sure you know this already. You have the right to remain silent. Anything you say can and will be used against you. You have the right to an attorney. If you can't afford an attorney one will be provided for you."

I was handcuffed and placed in the back of a squad car. I thought, this cannot be happening. It felt like one of those dreams professional people have where their most feared public humiliation comes true.

At the police station I told the cops that I was afraid to be in a cell with the other arrestees because I might have prosecuted some of them. No problem, I was told. Just sit in the waiting room.

They inventoried the contents of my wallet, took my mug shot, fingerprinted me—all the things that, like white people, I would know only from TV if I wasn't, in fact, a prosecutor. I didn't have any money for the pay phone, so my arresting officer gave me a quarter to make my proverbial phone call.

That's when the privilege kicked back in. I know so many lawyers it actually took me several minutes to decide which one to call. I chose Mark Srere, one of my best friends. Since I was to be taken downtown for "processing," he said he'd meet me there.

Two cops—male and female, both black—transported me to the courthouse. The only police officers who have ever given me breaks are African American women. By the end of the ride this one was on my side. I got her to read me the police report from my arrest file. She announced that she doubted the case would go anywhere. It's "he said, she said," and anyway, the arresting officer didn't follow procedure. He was supposed to call a supervisor before locking up someone from another law enforcement agency.

It was my first time walking through the prisoners' entrance at the courthouse. My handcuffs made it seem especially authentic. Normally, at the main entrance, I don't even have to go through the metal detectors. The U.S. marshals require defense attorneys to do that, but we prosecutors just show our ID's and breeze through. Not that day.

Inside the courthouse I was placed in a holding cell, alone. I was officially behind bars. My friend Renée Raymond, a public defender, came to see me. Apparently it was all over the courthouse that a prosecutor was locked up. Three lawyers volunteered to represent me.

Renée said that Michele Roberts, a black woman considered by many to be the best trial lawyer in the District of Columbia, was trying to get the case dropped. Everyone expected that this would happen, but they were proceeding cautiously to make it clear that I was not getting special treatment. Special treatment? I almost laughed.

In the meantime a guy from Pretrial Services came to interview me and take my urine sample for drug testing. Filling out his form, he asked me the highest grade I completed. I told him law school. He looked like he didn't believe it but dutifully wrote it down.

A few hours passed. The cell was so filthy I couldn't even sit on the metal bench. I just didn't trust those stains. I wondered what Senator Durenberger would have said if he could have seen me then.

Then lunchtime. A courthouse employee came in, looked at me like I was a piece of shit, and literally threw a paper bag through the bars of my cell. Lunch meat, of uncertain origin, on white bread, and an apple. I was not hungry.

Finally Michele Roberts arrived, with bad news: "I don't believe it, but they are going to prosecute this. You are going to be arraigned in a few minutes. They probably won't ask for bail. Let me do all the talking."

Thank God I didn't know the judge in arraignment court. I thought everybody would be staring at me, but nobody even looked interested. I was just one of the hundred black men on the lockup list that day. A trial date was set, the judge ordered me to stay away from Detroit, and I was free to leave. Michele gave me money for a cab, and finally, in the privacy of my home, I cried.

The next day, at work, was worse. I was the only black male prosecutor in my office and the only lawyer in the history of the section ever to have been arrested. Everybody knew. My boss at the Justice Department got a call from the U.S. attorney for the District of Columbia—the head of the office that was prosecuting me. There was no love lost between our two agencies.

The U.S. attorney reminded my boss that I prosecuted a case against a clerk in his office, a guy who was stealing film and then selling it. We had arranged a sting against him.

It was actually one of my favorite cases. We videotaped the guy offering to sell film to an undercover agent. He worked as a supply clerk in the prosecutor's office and said he could steal as much film as the undercover agent wanted. Under the law, the higher the dollar value of the crime, the more time the bad guy gets, so our agent strung this dude along, getting him to offer to sell more and more film. Every time the man offered to sell more, his sentence increased. When the perp got up to the quantity of film that could send him to jail for about twenty years, we arrested him, just to put an end to his self-destruction. Then we had a good laugh— what a dumb-ass.

Now the U.S. attorney was telling my boss that he sure would have liked to have known about that case in advance. It embarrassed him. And now here we were with the tables turned.

My boss was pissed—at them, not me. He kept me on all my cases, including the high-profile one against Senator Durenberger. "Just make sure you get a good lawyer," he said. I told him about Michele Roberts. Later the same day he called me into his office. He'd checked on her and said I'd made the right decision. She's the best.

The DC criminal court had so much business that it took fifteen long months to get to my trial. During the days I continued to put bad guys in jail. At night I worked with my lawyer and investigators to try to keep my ass out.

Finally, the day of reckoning. The bailiff calls the case: "The United States of America versus Paul Butler." No joke. I am very familiar with the phrasing; it's how all federal criminal cases are styled: the U.S. against the defendant. It's just that I never before had a reason to ponder how bizarre it sounds—you know, the most powerful nation in the history of the world against you. I think I could handle Rhode Island or North Dakota, maybe even the District of Columbia versus Paul, but the frigging United States of America! I feel a little overpowered.

The jury is ten blacks, two whites. The prosecutor who says he doesn't consider race when choosing jurors is either stupid or a liar. That's like the myth that lawyers want an impartial jury. Bullshit. Like any other lawyer, a prosecutor wants a jury that is predisposed to decide the case in favor of his client. In that equation, of course race makes a difference.

While virtually every criminal lawyer agrees that race matters, there are different schools of thought about how. Some of my fellow prosecutors believe that in your average black male defendant case, you try to avoid black male jurors. The fear is they'll be overly sympathetic. Others think just the opposite—a black man is just the juror you want, because he'll want to distinguish himself from this black man on trial. He'll prove he's different by voting to convict the defendant. It's similar to another theory that almost every prosecutor would endorse: women jurors are harder on female defendants (and even female victims) than they are on males.

In any event, my thoughts on this issue are irrelevant because Michele doesn't consult me. She's made it clear that she is the one in charge. In criminal court in DC, as in most other jurisdictions, both sides have "preemptory challenges" that allow them to exclude a few jurors for virtually any reason. Race actually isn't supposed to be one of the reasons, but it's an easy rule to get around. You just have to offer a "race neutral" reason. My favorite of these was in a case in which the defense claimed the prosecutor was striking Latinos. The prosecutor answered that it wasn't Latinos he was challenging, it was people who spoke Spanish. That case went all the way up to the Supreme Court, which agreed with the prosecution that it was a race-neutral explanation.

So it would have been easy for Michele to exclude them, but she allows a couple of young black men to stay in the jury pool. I don't know whether to throw them a black power salute or avoid their gaze. I just hope that I haven't prosecuted them for anything.

The prosecution calls its first witness: my arresting officer. The famed defense attorney Alan Dershowitz once claimed that 99 percent of police officers lie under oath. I don't know if it's that high, but every prosecutor has faced the situation of having to put a cop on the stand whose testimony is questionable. The relationship between the prosecutor and a lying police officer is more complicated than you'd think. On the one hand, you don't want to sponsor perjurious testimony. On the other hand, you don't want to get the cop mad at you for believing some defendant over him. So, unless you have compelling evidence that the officer is lying, you tend to go along to get along. Your conscience is absolved, however, because Dershowitz has another hypothesis prosecutors definitely endorse: that 99 percent of people accused of crimes are guilty.

The one time I am in a position to know absolutely whether a police officer is telling the truth, because I am the subject of his testimony, he lies through his teeth. My arresting officer claims that when he drove up, he saw me vandalizing Donna's car. Under oath, he testifies that I cursed him out and threatened Detroit, then told him that he couldn't arrest me because I worked for the Department of Justice.

On cross-examination, my lawyer asks him a series of questions he can't answer: Why were there no other witnesses who reported seeing me vandalize Donna's car—not even the other police officers who had arrived at the same time? Why, if I had damaged the car, hadn't he arrested me for destruction of property? Why would I have pushed Detroit and then run to the parking lot and start putting sawdust on Donna's car? The jury starts looking at me a little more sympathetically.

The next witness is Detroit. Now, while it should not matter to jurors that a witness is unattractive, it absolutely does.[2] When I was prosecuting misdemeanors, it was a commonplace that if you had a defendant charged with a drug possession offense, and the dude was a good-looking black man, DC jurors were not going to send him to jail. Detroit is so short and heavy that as she walks down the courtroom's aisle to the witness chair, she lists from side to side. The jurors look at her and then look at me. Score one for the defense.

As a prosecutor, you try to make your victims sympathetic, but sometimes that's harder than you might think. Victims are often as mistrustful of the system as the defendant, and it comes across in their testimony—even, or maybe especially, the testimony of pretend victims. On the stand, Detroit is belligerent, confused, and occasionally incoherent. She does not appear to tell the truth, even about tangential matters. She claims to be a teacher, but the school where she says she teaches denies this. She says that she is a special police officer, but again there are no official records to verify this. She says that she has no plans to sue me in civil court, but Michele produces a letter from the lawyer that she hired for just that purpose. She simply does not come across as a credible person. At the end of her testimony, the prosecutor asks for time to find more witnesses. He says that "the cross-examination was obviously very effective" and that the government case needs bolstering. The judge denies the motion; in misdemeanor court each judge has about six cases scheduled for trial every day, so there is no time for delay.

The prosecution's final witnesses are a boyfriend and girlfriend who live downstairs from Detroit. They hadn't seen or heard anything, but Detroit had told them that I assaulted her. If it is possible to have a favorite moment at your own criminal trial, here is mine. My lawyer asks Detroit's downstairs neighbor if he believed Detroit when she claimed that I had pushed her. His answer: "No. She lies about everything. I don't believe anything she says."

After this the prosecution announces that it rests its case. A juror gasps. Loudly.

From my professional point of view, it is one of the worst prosecutions I have ever seen. A very good prosecutor has the skills to convict some innocent people—not every single person, but some. In our private lives we have all been made to look guilty of some transgression that we didn't actually commit. An excellent trial lawyer can do that, not always enough to prove a case beyond a reasonable doubt, but enough to give the jury something to chew on. For the record, if I had been the prosecutor in my trial, the government's case would have been a lot stronger.

At home the next morning, as I prepare to take the stand in my own defense, I get dressed as if I am headed to the greatest performance of my life. Because I am. The only person who can mess this up now is me. If I get convicted of this crime—this stupid little misdemeanor—life as I know it is over.

When I raise my right hand and swear to tell the truth, the whole truth, and nothing but the truth, I get that surreal feeling again. This was never supposed to happen to me.

I look each jury member in the eye and I tell them the story. The apartment, the rented parking space, Detroit, the sawdust. With all my heart I resent being in this position, but it's not the jury's fault. It is the goddamned prosecutors' fault. When it is time for their stupid cross-examination, I let them have it. I am angry and self-righteous and I spit my answers. The U.S. attorney's office has devoted two lawyers to my case, including a senior black prosecutor. I hate him the most. I am just getting going when the judge announces a recess for lunch.

Michele has a stern look on her face. We find a corner in the hall where we can talk. She whispers that if I continue to respond in the same way, I am going to be found guilty and probably sentenced to prison. "Turn off the attitude and just answer the questions. You are too angry and it's coming across really badly. Like you did it."

That afternoon I am meek as a lamb. This seems to go over well. After my testimony, Donna takes the stand and tells the jury about Detroit's belligerence. Then, in a touch that I had arranged to stick it to the U.S. Attorney's Office, Michele calls two federal prosecutors as character witnesses. One is actually from the same office that is prosecuting me. He says that he cannot imagine me committing the crime with which his employer is accusing me. The defense rests, there are short closing statements, and the case goes to the jury.

The courthouse doesn't keep records of these things, but as far as anybody remembers, it is the shortest jury deliberation in Superior Court history. Less than ten minutes had elapsed from the time the jurors left the courtroom until the time they returned, and they had already gathered their coats and other belongings.

"Has the jury reached an unanimous verdict?" the judge asks.

"Yes," the forewoman says.

"Mr. Butler, please rise."

As Michele stands up with me, she touches my hand and whispers, "I did my best. You never know what a jury is going to do, but we gave it our best."

"What is the verdict of the jury?"

"Your Honor, we the jury find the defendant not guilty."

It is like a movie. I hug Michele, and my friends in the courtroom cheer. The Nazi-looking police officer stalks out of the courtroom like he's mad. The judge smiles at me and says, "Mr. Butler, you are free to go."

I want to say that the prosecutors hung their heads, but they probably just packed up and left. That's what I did when I lost a case. They certainly didn't apologize. I never did either when I got a "not guilty" verdict. Usually I blamed the jurors.

My story is different from those of most of the approximately 14 million Americans who get arrested every year.[3] I had the best defense attorney in the city, because I could afford her. I knew how to appeal to a jury—hell, I'd prosecuted folks in the very courtroom where I was being prosecuted. In addition to carefully preparing my testimony, I made sure that my haircut was conservative and my shoes were shined. I knew how to look like the kind of African American a jury would not want to send to jail.

I was innocent. By the way. During the process, that fact seemed rather beside the point. Our criminal justice system works like a meat grinder. You are supposed to proceed, in orderly fashion, from arrest to guilty plea to sentencing. More than 90 percent of criminal cases are resolved just that way.

During the period between my arrest and trial, I kept feeling pressure to go along with the program. The prosecutor told my lawyer that I was eligible for "diversion"—a program for first-time offenders of minor crimes in which the charges are dismissed if you do community service. "I'm sure he does community service already" was the line repeated to me.

I actually considered it. However, my boss at the Department of Justice, a red-faced Irishman who looked more like a beat cop than a top government official, said, "If you take diversion, everybody will think you are guilty." That was all I needed to hear. I wanted my day in court.

The system worked for me—to the extent that you can describe a system as "working" when a man is arrested and made to stand trial for a crime he did not commit. At least I was not convicted, which makes me as grateful for my money, my defense attorney, my social standing, my connections, and my legal skills as for my actual innocence.

A few months after my acquittal, I left the Justice Department. People ask if I stopped being a prosecutor because I had been prosecuted myself. I deny it, but let's get real. What I mean by saying "no" is that I wasn't forced out. I was in the middle of preparing the biggest case in the office and my boss would have preferred that I stay. Still, I was the junior lawyer on the case, and there was enough time before the senator's trial for someone else to be brought up to speed.

Also, not long after my trial the senator's case got transferred to Minnesota, which was his home state. It became, let's say, less important to have an African American prosecutor on the case there than in DC. As it happened, the case never went to trial at all. The senator ended up pleading guilty. To misdemeanors.

It sounds silly, but what I remember most about my own case is how mean some people were. The police officer who lied on the stand. The guy who threw the lunch bag at me inside my cell. My landlord, who refused to get involved with the case even though he had also had run-ins with Detroit.

There are still some hard-core types in the U.S. attorney's office who don't speak to me. I say to hell with them because, truth be told, I am still a little angry also.

So now I describe myself as a recovering prosecutor—"recovering" because one never quite gets over it. I still like to point my finger at the bad guy. I get really angry at people who victimize others. The creep who snatches the old lady's purse—I would like to kick his ass myself. And the monster who molests little kids—I want him *under* the jail. I don't have a problem with the law reflecting those passions. It should.

But I am scared of what can happen when those feelings get out of control. My sense of justice always has been big and bulging. What my own personal prosecution expanded is my sense of injustice.

Sometimes I still hate the woman who falsely accused me. She tried to destroy me. I was innocent. Really. Maybe you don't completely believe me either. That's another effect of my prosecution. I'm not as innocent as I was before. I have a record.

We need our criminal justice system to understand. Detroit? She did a terrible thing. That is different, however, from saying that we should respond as if she is a terrible human being. She appears to have serious mental health issues. She thought she had to get back at a pompous lawyer who ruined her little part-time hustle. She needed something validated, and she did what she thought she had to do. She's pathetic more than she's evil.

What she did could have destroyed a less privileged person. As for me, I kept my job, my friends, most of my social status. In some ways the experience was useful. It made a man out of me—a black man. I now share a bond with lots of people from whom I used to feel somewhat disconnected.

Those are the places I let myself go. I don't dwell too long on other stuff because it still hurts. I never told my mother. She'll find out when she reads this. In the African American community, it's a big thing when a mom can brag that she "never had to go to the courthouse." I don't doubt that my mother would have been incredibly supportive and sympathetic. Ma's got no love for the police. She still quakes with anger when she talks about the time my stepfather, then about sixty-five, got into a minor car accident with a vehicle driven by a white man, and the cops ordered my stepfather to get in the backseat of the squad car while they talked to the white driver. Still, if Ma had known, she would have insisted on coming to my trial and I could not have had that. I have seen too many black mothers, seated in the courtroom in the row behind their sons, crying. I did not want to see my mother in that place. I would prefer that her memory of Superior Court be of me in trial, not on trial.

I don't know what I am ashamed of. I do know that my arrest and prosecution hurt me in ways I still haven't touched. And probably never will.

We need our justice system to understand all of that.

A conservative, famously, is a liberal who gets mugged. What is a prosecutor who is arrested and tried for a crime that he did not commit? It may be tempting to interpret the rest of this book—which indicts American criminal justice—as an elaborate exercise in revenge. My goal, however, is more ambitious. I am still a prosecutor at heart. I like justice and fair play. It turns out that we don't have a lot of either in our criminal justice system right now. This book is about how to get them back. My main concern is you—the law-abiding person. I want to keep you safe and free.

The next chapter will discuss how mass incarceration and the expansion of police power impact the lives of the ordinary citizen. The focus will be on public safety. There is a tipping point at which crime increases if too many people are incarcerated. The United States is past this point. If we lock up fewer people, we will be safer.

Chapter 3 examines the sordid impact of the War on Drugs—

the hypocrisy, the futility, but mainly the future. One way to make everyone safer and more free would be to end that war. Doing so would dramatically reduce both the prison population and the rate of violent crime. But how would this work? Would people be able to buy cocaine at Whole Foods? Let's think about the benefit of treating narcotics with remedies other than criminal law and the surprising public safety benefits that might come with this approach.

Jurors have an unusual power to help end mass incarceration. This book explains the doctrine of jury nullification—an extraordinary tool provided by the Constitution to every juror in every criminal case but one that modern-day judges try to keep secret. I will recommend a way that jurors can use this hidden power to make their communities safer and send a strong message for change to politicians and prosecutors. Strategic jury nullification has the potential to revolutionize American criminal justice.

The American criminal justice system is so dysfunctional that it presents well-intentioned people with a dilemma. Should good people cooperate with it? This book looks at the roles of two actors without whom the justice system would grind to a halt: snitches and prosecutors. A debate rages in both pop culture and criminology about the value of snitches. I come down firmly on the side against them. Government informants are the seedy underbelly of the criminal justice system. I'll talk about the addiction of law enforcement to snitches and the devastating impact they have on neighborhoods and civil liberties.

My experiences as a prosecutor persuade me that prosecutors are more part of the problem than the solution. Many mean well, but the "lock 'em up" culture is so pervasive that it defeats even people with the best of intentions. Chapter 6, "Should Good People Be Prosecutors?" explains how that culture defeated me. Any advocate for change who wonders whether he or she can do more good working on the inside should find this section useful. The answer, usually, is "no."

The end of the book imagines a better world, focusing on ways that both pop culture and technology can make a difference. Hip-hop music contains a powerful analysis of the criminal justice system by the people who know it from the inside out. Chapter 7, "A Hip-Hop Theory of Justice," demonstrates how the most thuggish of art forms points to more effective law and order.

New technology is often viewed as a threat to freedom. Yet scientific developments, handled with care, have as much potential to free us as to oppress us. The book takes a look at the most exciting new advances, focusing on how they can make us more secure and, at the same time, reduce our reliance on police power and incarceration.

I conclude by recommending seven interventions that will make us safer and freer. There is reason to be cautiously optimistic that we can reverse the drift toward an American police state, but we must be thoughtful and we must act now. The freedom we save will be our own.

2

Safety First:
Why Mass Incarceration Matters

I became a prosecutor because I hate bullies. I stopped being a prosecutor because I hate bullies.

When people are treated unfairly, I get itching mad. Part of my anger is based on an acute sense of justice. I was raised by a single mom who marched with Martin Luther King Jr. She was patriotic, in her way. In our segregated neighborhood we were the only family that hung the flag on the Fourth of July. We loved the idea of America; we just didn't see it reflected much around us. "All we want," Martin Luther King Jr. said, "is what you put on paper."

Another part of my desire to help the downtrodden is not so righteous. Like a lot of prosecutors, I possess a zeal that can border on the bloodthirsty. I am the Avenger of the hood. My mother also fancied Malcolm X, the African American revolutionary. His heroes, he said, were "people who bled for freedom, and who made others bleed."

When I joined the United States Department of Justice I was detailed to the criminal court of the District of Columbia, prosecuting people for drug and gun crimes. I put a lot of people in prison, and I had a great time doing it. Not only was I doing the Lord's work, I was assigned the fun part of His job description — the wrathful, vengeful, angry part.

Did part of my satisfaction stem from my own life story? When you are a black kid attending a lousy public school on the South Side of Chicago and you get good test scores and you talk like a white boy, you get beat up sometimes—by other black boys with not-so-good test scores who don't end up at the prosecutor's table. Years later you might see boys who look like them at the defendant's table in the courtroom, and you—the prosecutor—point your finger at them and call them names. It is part of your job. This is justice, too, the poetic kind.

My friends from law school thought it was kind of wack that I was a prosecutor. I had been the down-for-the-cause brother who they had expected to work for Legal Aid or as a public defender. I told them I was helping people in the most immediate way— delivering the protection of the law to communities that needed it most, making the streets safer, and restoring to victims some measure of the dignity that a punk criminal had tried to steal. I actually believed that then.

I don't anymore. I still love the idea of America; I just do not see it reflected in our dysfunctional system of criminal justice. We are neither as safe nor as free as we could be. We have moved far away from the bedrock principles of liberty and fair play. The founders would be most aggrieved by the current state of affairs (after getting over the shock of my being the messenger of the bad news). Look what we've done to their revolution.

May 2008. In a high-crime neighborhood in DC, the police stop every driver on a public street. You are required to answer whether you have a "legitimate purpose" for being in the neighborhood. Those purposes, according to police regulations, include going to church, seeing a doctor, or visiting family. If the police officer decides that you do not have a legitimate purpose, you are ordered to leave the neighborhood. If you refuse, you are arrested for the crime of "failure to obey a police officer." Defending the plan, Cathy Lanier, the DC police chief, says, "In certain areas we need to go beyond the normal methods of policing."[1]

Any random day: I am riding in a police car with my friend Sgt. Brett Jones (not his real name), of the Washington, DC, Metropolitan Police Department. We are playing "Stop that Car!" It's a game he invented, to show off. It's just as it sounds: I pick a car—any car—and he stops it. Most often I select an expensive car, a Mercedes or BMW, driven by some guy in a suit.

Sgt. Jones is a good cop. He waits until he has a legal reason to stop the car. It doesn't take long, never more than three or four blocks of following. There are so many potential traffic infractions that it is impossible to drive without committing one. This gives Sgt. Jones an extraordinary amount of power. He can stop anybody he wants. Then comes the questioning, followed sometimes by the order to get out of the car, the pat down, the flashlight search inside the car, the request to open the trunk, the call for backup.

We have, for the last thirty years, locked up more and more people each year. The incarceration rate increases seemingly without regard to the crime rate. When crime goes up, we lock up more people. When crime goes down, we lock up more people. When the crime rate stays the same, we lock up more people.

At this rate, in the future, everyone will go to jail for fifteen days. In the name of safety, American citizens will be treated like criminals. Every move we make in public will be recorded. In private we will be expected to watch and report on each other.

Minor infractions (spitting on a sidewalk, crossing a street against the light, not recycling the trash, forgetting to put on a seat belt, drinking in public) will be treated like affronts to the state. The police will have vast power to search our bodies, homes, and property. They will arrest on the slightest provocation.

Millions will be locked up. Millions more than now, which is 2.3 million. Now, the United States has the largest rate of incarceration in the history of the free world.

To avoid going further down this terrible road there are two things we must do. First, we must be smarter about what makes us safe. There is nothing wrong with wanting to be secure. The problem is that the way that we are going about it is counterproductive.

If we respond more rationally, and lock up fewer people, we will actually be safer.

Second, we must stop being so afraid. To live in a free country is to tolerate a minimum level of risk. The framers thought that freedom was worth this cost. In the Bill of Rights, they struck a balance between individual liberty and state power. When we return to the best values of the patriots—their trust in the common person and their suspicion of an overbearing government—we will live up to democracy's highest ideals.

The biggest threat to freedom in the United States comes not from some foriegn or terrorist threat but rather from our dysfunctional criminal justice system. It is out of control. We define too many acts as crimes, punish too many people far longer than their crimes warrant, and therefore have too much incarceration. Some people deserve to be in jail, but not two million—as I will explain, we could reduce that number at least 25 percent and actually be safer. There are better ways to address problems—solutions that will make families and communities whole, and treat people who have made mistakes more humanely.

The two million Americans in prison represent the most urgent challenge to democratic values since the civil rights era. If we fail to respond, our country will become a police state in which the way of life of all citizens is eroded. If we act thoughtfully, however, the United States can not only be saved but also improved, just as the civil rights movement ultimately benefited everybody, not just minorities.

INCARCERATION NATION:
THE FACTS

Prison is supposed to be where we put the most dangerous people. If that is true, something apparently made U.S. citizens turn degenerate during the 1980s and 1990s, something requiring quadrupling the percentage of citizens we incarcerate. For the prior fifty years the incarceration rate had remained relatively stable.

Then, beginning in 1980, it exploded. The United States witnessed the largest expansion of a prison population in the history of the free world. The result:

- Today, 2.3 million people are in prison in the United States.[2]
- The United States has 5 percent of the world's population and 25 percent of its prisoners.[3]
- There are 60 percent more people in U.S. prisons than in the U.S. military.
- The state of California alone has more prisoners than do France, Great Britain, Germany, Japan, Singapore, and the Netherlands combined.
- In Baltimore, Maryland—population 615,000—115,000 people were arrested in one year.[4]
- Under the law of fifteen states, you can be sentenced to life imprisonment for a first-time, nonviolent marijuana offense. People are currently serving life sentences in the United States for marijuana crimes.[5]
- By 2011, the number of Americans under criminal justice supervision will be nearly eight million. That is equal to the combined populations of Los Angeles, Chicago, and Philadelphia.[6]
- In the United States one new prison or jail opens every week.[7]

STREET LAW FOR PATRIOTS

As the prison population exploded, police power also expanded dramatically. Of course, law enforcement must have the appropriate resources to keep citizens safe, but in a democracy we must always be vigilant that government agents do not become too powerful. The American Revolution was, in large part, a protest against excessive police power.

"Can the police do that?" Lawyers get asked that question a lot, especially when someone is watching a cop show like *Law &*

Order or *CSI*. The answer, frequently, is yes. Here, according to recent decisions of the United States Supreme Court, are some of the things that police can do:

- The police can lie to you. They can falsely claim that they have evidence when they don't, or that witnesses identified you, or that your friends have implicated you. They can even lie about lying—by saying that you failed a lie detector test when you did not. The police can lie about whether you have been charged with a crime, or how much time you could get for the crime with which you have been charged. They can tell you that you will be executed even if the crime they have charged you with carries no death penalty.
- The police can arrest you for a minor traffic offense like not wearing a seat belt or driving with expired tags. They can handcuff you and take you to jail even if the traffic offense itself carries no jail time. The Supreme Court recently held that it is constitutional for the police to make arrests for crimes that are punishable, upon conviction, only with fines.[8]
- If the police start chasing you, and you, in fleeing them, cause a danger to them or others, they can shoot you down or force your car to go over a cliff. In 2007 the Supreme Court said that Atlanta police acted constitutionally when they rammed a car off the road and down an incline. The driver had refused to stop after the police tried to pull him over. His subsequent injuries left him a quadriplegic. The crime that occasioned the high-speed chase? Speeding.[9]
- The police can detain you if they believe you are trying to avoid them in a high-crime neighborhood, even if they have no reason to suspect that you committed a crime. They can force you to stop just to investigate why you don't want to talk to them.[10]
- The police can ask to search your body or possessions or car without telling you that you have the right to say no. The

Supreme Court has ruled that citizens can provide "valid consent" to a search even when they don't know they are entitled to refuse.[11]

- When the police want to look inside a car but have no constitutional authority for a search, they can follow the driver for as long as it takes to observe a traffic offense—even a minor infraction like waiting too long at a stop sign or having air freshener dangling from the car's rearview mirror (that's illegal in most states). Once they observe the infraction, they can stop the car even if the only purpose is to inspect it, and even if they admit that they ordinarily wouldn't stop a driver for that infraction.[12]

- In most states, the police can stop you based in part on "racial incongruity," i.e. seeing you in a place where they don't normally see people of your race. In most of the country, racial profiling is legal. The police admit that they do it, and courts routinely approve of it as a legitimate law enforcement tactic.[13]

WHY WE SHOULD CARE: PUBLIC SAFETY

No reasonable person should be troubled when violent criminals go to prison. Nobody should have a problem with police having adequate authority and resources to keep us safe. But punishment has to be fair. If it is not, every member of society pays the price.

Why should the law-abiding citizen be concerned about the number of people in prison? Self-interest. Locking up too many people for nonviolent offenses has a negative impact on the quality of your life. Even if you set aside moral or political intuition, you should care about the number of people in prison if you want to feel more secure while in your home or walking down the street.

First, some statistics:

Inmates to be released from prison in 2008: 700,000
Inmates released in 2008 who will be arrested again by 2011: 469,000

Inmates with substance abuse problems: 75 percent
Inmates who are treated for substance abuse problems while
     in prison: 20 percent
Inmates in prison now who will eventually be released:
     95 percent[14]

Who is the typical inmate? Erase your mind's image of a violent predator. The majority of people who are locked up have committed nonviolent offenses—at least when they first go in. Picture the guy who works in the mailroom at your office, and the men who dry off your vehicle at the car wash, and the sweaty kids who came to your house to deliver the mattress. Think of your high school classmate, the dude who didn't quite make it to graduation but who you got to know a little bit because he sold you weed. Maybe he wouldn't be your ideal companion for lunch at the Four Seasons or your first choice to marry your daughter. But he's not exactly a menace to society. He's made some bad choices, done some stupid things, but he's still young and his life is still salvageable. Spiritual folks might say, "God is not through with him yet."

Now the question to ask is *How does locking this guy up help me?* Since it's very expensive—as a taxpayer you provide his room and board for the period of his incarceration—presumably you want to get some bang for your buck. Obviously it depends on what crime he committed. If someone is going to hurt or steal from others, then he belongs in jail. But for at least 500,000 people locked up right now, that's not the case.

As a matter of fact, nonviolent offenders are more likely to victimize you after they come out than they were before they went in. The odds are stacked against inmates leaving prison as better people. Most don't get reformed. It's not because they can't be rehabilitated, but rather because we use prison for a different purpose. It is a "correctional facility" in name only; "long-term storage locker" would be a more accurate description.

But aren't we better off if a bunch of dope boys are off the street? Maybe not. There are serious consequences to exposing a large group of nonviolent offenders to violent ones. Any parent who has cautioned her child against playing with the "bad" kids is familiar with the concern. Prison becomes a finishing school in criminal activity for nonviolent offenders—it is where they have the time and the eager teachers to learn how to be really good crooks. Good meaning bad.

THE TIPPING POINT

Change in violent crime in New York since 2000: –20 percent
Change in the New York State prison population since 2000: –14 percent

Change in violent crime in all other states since 2000: –1 percent
Change in the prison population of all other states since 2000: +12 percent

States that reduced prison populations while reducing crime: Connecticut, New Jersey, Ohio, and Massachusetts[15]

If we understand that the primary purpose of prison is public safety, we will get serious about ending mass incarceration, because it is counterproductive.

During the 1990s, crime rates went down. The interesting thing is that the crime rates fell everywhere, both in parts of the country that reduced their prison population and in those that saw huge increases in the prison population. An obvious conclusion is that crime rates are not directly related to incarceration rates. One category of crime that did go up, however, was offenses committed by former inmates. This suggests that the higher rates of incarceration were not a deterrent and may in fact have produced more criminals.[16]

The relationship between crime and prison is complicated.

Prison time doesn't exactly prevent crime and it doesn't exactly
cause crime. Its public safety benefit depends on our ability to cal-
ibrate how much to use it. The way we use prison now is tragically
off course.

Here's what we know. Incarceration lowers the crime rate to a
point. Most scholars believe that the increase in incarceration in
the 1990s lowered the crime rate by around 20 percent. It's hard to
know for sure, because crime declined even in jurisdictions that
didn't lock up so many people.

After that, most criminologists agree, the crime reduction benefit of incarceration levels off. Criminologists refer to this as "dimin-
ished returns."[17] What happens if, after this point, people continue
to get locked up at the same rate? The best evidence suggests
there's a tipping point—the moment at which there are so many
people in prison that crime actually increases.[18]

The tipping point theory first seems counterintuitive, but it's
not hard to understand. There are a couple of factors at work. First,
we simply cannot lock up all the potential criminals—say, all the
drug sellers. For every person who goes to jail (typically in reference to drug trafficking and prostitution), a vacancy is created that
at least one more person fills.[19] This "replacement effect" explains
why certain crimes remain stable no matter how many people we
lock up. But when the tipping point is reached, things actually get
worse. Why?

A second factor comes into play here. We know that the social
organization of neighborhoods has a far greater impact on community safety than any police strategy or prison term. When parents take care of their kids, neighbors look out for neighbors, and
communities are filled with working families, people are safest.
Mass incarceration upsets this dynamic in three ways.

First, it disrupts families. The legal anthropologist Donald Braman has described the family members of inmates, mainly women
and children, as "doing time on the outside."[20] At least half of the
men in prison have kids, as do an even larger percentage of incar-

cerated women.[21] Kids who grow up with a parent locked up are seven times more likely to get locked up themselves.[22]

Second, too much incarceration creates too many unemployable young men. My mother looks with disdain at the guys hanging out on the street corner. Many of these young men have served time. Now they seem idle. Mom asks the classic question: "Why don't they just get a job at McDonald's?"

It turns out that it's actually hard to get a job at McDonald's.[23] It's hard for a high school dropout, who's maybe thirty years old and has a ten-year gap in his résumé, to get a job anywhere. Frankly, if I had a choice between hiring him and some fresh-faced nineteen-year-old who's a student at a community college, the ex-con wouldn't be my first choice either. If I feel this way—and I am an advocate of criminal justice reform—imagine how the manager down at Starbucks feels. He is willing to give a guy a break, but hiring a former inmate seems like too much of a risk. Now multiply this impact by 700,000—the number of ex-cons who get released in an average year. The odds are against successful reentry into civil society.

Finally, mass incarceration changes the way that people think about crime and punishment. In some low-income communities, going to jail has become a rite of passage. Young men expect that at some point they are going to do some time and, statistically, they are correct. People have less respect for the law, for the police, and ultimately for each other. The criminal law protects us only when going to prison is a stigma that folks try to avoid. If you *expect* to do some time, the deterrent effect of the criminal law disappears. Yet the policy of mass incarceration creates the reasonable expectation that many people are going to go to prison. It becomes a self-fulfilling prophecy. From a law-and-order perspective, when citizens begin to think getting locked up is normal, disaster looms. Welcome to the future—unless we act quickly and decisively to reverse course.

FIVE MORE REASONS

$60 Billion

Sixty billion dollars is the amount that the United States spends on prisons and jails every year.[24] This does not include the costs of police and the courts. If the United States lowered its incarceration rates to that of most other industrialized nations, we would have billions more dollars every year to devote to health care, education, and the environment. One reason European nations are able to provide more social services to their citizens is that they do not spend nearly as much money on prisons as we do. It isn't that their citizens are more law-abiding; they are not.[25] These countries simply lock up fewer people and for less time. And, for the record, you are safer walking at night on the streets of Paris or Berlin than you are in the average American city.[26]

The point is that government budgets are a zero-sum game. Money that goes to more prison beds has to come from somewhere else. California has some of the best public universities in the nation. Now, however, you can directly chart the money leaving the education system and going toward prison expenditures. Soon that state will spend more money on prisons than on colleges.[27] Vermont, Michigan, Oregon, Connecticut, and Delaware already do.[28] Bill Shiebler, president of the University of California Student Association, said, "A budget is a statement of priorities. It seems they're more interested in locking people up than giving people an opportunity in life."[29]

Civil Liberties

When we compare rates of incarceration around the world, the United States is in bad company. Russia has rates closest to ours, but our rate continues to rise even as the Russian rate has begun to decline.[30] The democracies of Western Europe imprison far fewer of their citizens.[31] There are, for example, more people locked up in the United States for drug crimes alone than for all crimes in the entire European Union.[32] And the EU has almost 200 million more people than the United States! While it is still fair to describe the United States as a "free" country, we are not nearly as free as we once were given the percentage of our citizens who are locked up. We are not as free as any other industrial democracy in the world.

Some people consider it unpatriotic to question police power. These people must be ignorant of American history. The men who wrote the Constitution were frankly distrustful of law enforcement. The Bill of Rights intentionally makes it harder for the police to do their jobs. It sets high standards for when the police can search, or for the kinds of questions they can force you to answer. The framers recognized that enforcing the criminal law is not an absolute value. Excessive law enforcement was seen as a greater threat than the guilty going free.

That is one reason the Bill of Rights includes the Fifth Amendment's radical privilege against self-incrimination. If you are guilty of a crime, you don't have to report on yourself. What a brave concept that is—an idea so radical that it has not been adopted by many other countries. Even some European nations do not have a privilege against self-incrimination. The amendment expresses the supreme confidence in liberty—the right to be left alone—that our Constitution embodies.

When citizens are very afraid, they do not value their rights as much.[33] They are willing to trade freedom for security. They believe that the government has to be very strong to keep them safe, and they expect this will involve some diminution of their civil liberties.

Ironically, the Supreme Court has interpreted the Constitution in a way that means that these low expectations become a self-fulfilling prophecy. The Fourth Amendment puts limits on the government's ability to invade our privacy. But the Court, in *Katz v. United States*, said that if the government intrusion is in an area

in which we don't *expect* privacy in the first place, there is no violation.[34] So constitutionally speaking we have only as much privacy as we expect.

Under this doctrine, if the president said, "My fellow Americans, the police will be watching you all the time from now on,"
and we believed it, the next day the police could break into our
homes and look in our computers and under our mattress. They
would not have violated the Constitution because we no longer
expected privacy. This test has been much criticized. Even Justice
John Harlan, who created it, later said it was a mistake—but it is
still the law of the land.[35]

What it means is that in order to protect ourselves against a police state we have to have high expectations. We have to be vigilant. In addition to not fearing the bad guys, we must not fear the
police.

When the Supreme Court ruled that gay people couldn't be
punished for consensual sex, it waxed eloquent about a right to liberty in its "more transcendent dimensions."[36] There is something
beautiful about a land where people are free to run down the street
for no reason at all. If we make everything that is "deviant" a crime,
eventually we all become criminals. In a free country people need
lots of leeway to be themselves, with the obvious caveat that they
must not hurt others. When we have over three thousand courses
of conduct that we've defined as criminal, and more than two million people in prison, we are not free enough.

Race Relations

Disparity in unemployment between blacks and whites:
   2 to 1
Disparity in unwed births between blacks and whites: 3 to 1
Disparity in incarceration between blacks and whites: 8 to 1

By midcentury, people of color will be a majority of the population
of the United States. How are we all going to get along? In no as-

pect of American life are differences between blacks and whites as extreme as they are in incarceration. One in every three young African American men has a criminal case—he's either in prison, on probation or parole, or awaiting trial. A young black man has a 32 percent chance of going to prison. A young white man has a 6 percent chance.[37]

Freedom has a special resonance for African Americans. Slavery limited their liberty; it was a way of controlling blacks. Now prison serves the same function. It causes many African Americans to harbor strong feelings of resentment against the government. Indeed, "hate" would not be too strong a word to describe the feeling in some urban communities toward the criminal justice system and the police—the most visible agents of the state.

The fear of African Americans that their government is overbearing and unresponsive is similar to the concerns of the original American patriots. Reducing incarceration and police power is rooted in an affirmation of the great American experiment—and a way to extend its ideals of liberty and fair play to every citizen. If we solve these problems, our democracy will be stronger.

To say that racial disparities in criminal justice engender animosity among blacks is not to imply any particular solution to the problem. It's not about holding blacks to lower standards; it's about applying the criminal law fairly. African Americans don't need more punishment than whites for crimes both groups commit at the same rates, but that's the reality of our criminal justice system now. If we reduce the number of Americans in prison, blacks will benefit disproportionately. If we make the streets safer, blacks—now most likely to be victims of crime—will also benefit disproportionately. Other parts of this book will make the argument that these are achievable goals. Here, I just want to note that mass incarceration is disastrous for race relations, and when it is gone, so too will be a major source of African Americans' disenchantment with their citizenship. They will be more a part of the fabric of America and they will certainly be freer.

Good Government

To have the most effective criminal justice policy, we should listen more to the experts. Our criminal justice policy is often inefficient, sometimes counterproductive. It is frequently driven by emotion rather than logic.

The federal sentencing disparity between crack cocaine and powder cocaine possession and/or distribution is a revealing example. In 1986 an African American college basketball player named Len Bias died of a cocaine overdose. Bias had been drafted to play with the Boston Celtics. Tip O'Neill, the Speaker of the House, represented Boston in Congress and took Bias's death especially hard. O'Neill decided to use it as an opportunity to show that the Democrats were as tough on crime as the Republicans were. At the time, possession of crack cocaine, which is made by cooking powder cocaine together with baking soda, was punished like possession of any other form of the drug. O'Neill decided that it should be punished on roughly a one to twenty-five ratio—i.e., one would get the same punishment for possession of one gram of crack that one got for twenty-five grams of powder. The Republicans, not wanting to be outdone on "their" issue of criminal justice, upped the ante closer to a one-to-fifty ratio. O'Neill countered with a disparity ratio near one to seventy-five. The spitting contest ended up at one to a hundred, which is the present law of the land. There was no scientific evidence presented at the hearings that *any* disparity was warranted, much less one set at one to a hundred.

Years later, after both crack and the crack disparity had ravaged low-income families, the United States Sentencing Commission recommended that Congress get rid of the disparity. Both presidents Clinton and Bush were in favor of equalizing crack and powder sentences as well. Congress has refused. Politicians are still afraid of being made to look "soft on crime."

The ironic punch line to this episode? An autopsy revealed that Len Bias didn't die from crack cocaine. He overdosed on powder.

For twenty years prosecutors have enforced a law that has wreaked havoc on families, that every recent president has opposed, that the federal sentencing commissioners—the experts appointed by Congress to recommend sentences—say is indefensible, and for which there is no scientific support. Yet it remains the law of the land. Stories like this are all too common in criminal justice.

In a democracy, people have the right to make bad law, within constitutional limitations. Criminal law, unfortunately, has been marred by runaway populism. We would be wary of being the driving force behind law about nuclear power or food safety. In good government there is a balance between democracy and expertise, between common sense and science. In criminal justice, we get the balance wrong, with tragic consequences.

The Right Thing to Do

If the soul of a nation is revealed by how it treats its prisoners, we have a lot of work to do. As a federal prosecutor I visited prisons all over the United States. In the main they are violent and cruel.

We seem to prefer them that way. During the 1990s we started to take away anything that might make time in the cages bearable—television, exercise equipment, and then, stupidly, opportunities for education.[38] When we lock up so many people—especially so many poor people and minorities—and then treat them like garbage, we tell on ourselves. The economist Glenn Loury has described the "expressive function" of incarceration: it creates a "national narrative about who is to blame for the maladies that beset our troubled civilization."[39]

To state the obvious, there are a number of bad things about our society for which people in prison are not responsible. Most prisoners are the victims of other "crimes" like poverty, lack of health care, and miserable schools. This is not to say that they don't belong in prison—many absolutely do. But we want to make sure that in addition to anger and revenge we also show

mercy, forgiveness, and compassion. According to the spiritual tra-
ditions of many Americans, we even should love the criminal—
not her crime, but her humanity. This is a tall order, to be sure, but
morality never was supposed to be an easy proposition. Thus for all
the practical reasons it will be useful to end mass incarceration—
including that the country will be safer, more free, in much better
economic shape, and less vulnerable to civil unrest—there's another reason: it's the right thing to do.

3

Justice on Drugs

When I became a prosecutor I promised myself that I would not smoke marijuana anymore.

It was not a hard promise to keep. It had never been a regular thing. And it would have been slightly discordant to spend a day working up a frothy-mouthed closing statement about why this particular drug dealer ought to be locked up, and then go home and fire up a joint.

Still, that wasn't the strongest incentive. I could have rationalized that—prosecutors learn to live with flexible standards. They get comfortable with a certain arbitrariness in the allocation of justice. So the work didn't really present an ethical barrier to a hit every now and then.

There was a more practical roadblock. The Justice Department requires all of its criminal lawyers to submit to random piss tests. I wasn't about to lose my good government job over some weed. My pot smoking had always been occasional and recreational, not something that was a big deal or that I thought I would miss. It was simply expected by those in the circles in which I traveled. Working in the prosecutor's office was the first time in my life that I was around a lot of highly educated young people who did not use illegal drugs. (I should note, though, that prosecutors are the hardest-drinking folks I've ever known.)

Some of my fondest memories of Yale and Harvard involve being drunk or stoned, or trying to get that way. In my third year of law school, when I was supposed to be in Administrative Law, I instead looked for Ecstasy. I had a keen sense of the romance of the hunt. What a fantastic name for a consumer product! How could you not want to find Ecstasy?

Any honest consideration of drugs ought to acknowledge the pleasures of intoxication. I remember Amsterdam, with Susan: we had space cakes, and then took the tram, which turned into a flying carpet. We laughed so hard; we were stupid happy. It is one of the top ten memories of my life, a memory made even sweeter now that Susan is gone. I remember a conference with some famous law professors and some magic mushrooms (interesting combination, that). Listening to music, we did something that academics never do: we shut up. We each chose a song to play. Someone put on Nina Simone's "Lilac Wine." After she sang the last wistful note, we opened our eyes and looked at each other in wonder: can you believe all this beauty in the world? I have never experienced the communion of saints, but thanks to a psychedelic drug, I have communed with a bunch of middle-aged professors. The experience was, I am embarrassed to admit, sublime.

These are the things that science knows, and that you know, but that never seem to come up in the public policy discussion. Some drugs are big fun. Most people who get high are not addicts. Lots of lovely people indulge. For these reasons we are never going to prevent folks from using drugs. It's impossible.

I could list the many bad things about drugs, but they already frame the conversation. Some addicts steal to support their habit. Every family has an alcoholic. Rehab is possible but quite difficult. Narcotics have utterly laid waste to some people's lives. For Wayne, from law school, weed was his gateway drug to weed. Too much weed, weed to get out of bed in the morning, weed to go to sleep at night. I guess he is what you call a high-functioning addict: he maintains his sophisticated labor law practice but he does not maintain his friends. One fall we traveled to France. Wayne had the good sense not to bring the stuff on the airplane, but once in Paris he had to have it, "had to" with an intensity that would put a crackhead to shame. Like a fool, I went with him to the Arab quarter to help him find some smoke. It was two months after September 11, 2001, and the police, with submachine guns, were everywhere, but that did not stop dark young men from whispering "hashish" or Wayne from following one of them down a serpentine alley to try to score some. I was vexed, and scared, and then — when Wayne reemerged from the alley alive — grateful, but I never wanted to travel with Wayne again. It's not really an option, anyway; he's now lost contact with all his friends.

Even if the science says that only a small percentage of drug users are addicts, or that drugs themselves don't cause people to act violently, these are the nightmare images that inform our analysis and our criminal law, even when we should know better.

My friend Edgar lives in Harlem. I tell him that I don't think drugs should be criminalized. He disagrees. He rails about the price his community paid during the 1980s crack epidemic. He summons up memories of blood in the street. He thinks those guys should all be put in prison.

Of course, when I walk into Edgar's apartment, the marijuana haze is so thick it is hard to breathe. I am more worried about his lungs than his brain. I don't regard his hypocrisy as evidence of irrationality. Edgar has simply absorbed the propaganda. In his talk, if not his walk, he's just another soldier in the War on Drugs.

Like I was. It wasn't until after I quit the war that I saw the carcasses.

A BRIEF HISTORY OF DRUG PROHIBITION: OPIUM-SNIFFING CHINAMEN, COCAINIZED NEGROES, AND CRAZY MEXICANS

For most of the history of the United States, drugs have been legal. In the nineteenth century you could walk into your local apothecary and purchase opium, cocaine, or marijuana. A number of women became addicted to "patent medicine," which they took for menstrual pain and which contained up to 50 percent morphine.

Many veterans of the Union army also got hooked on morphine after taking it for injuries they got fighting the Civil War.

In part to resolve the addiction problem, which afflicted between 2 percent and 5 percent of the adult population, Congress, in 1906, passed its best drug law ever. Significantly, it was not a criminal law. The Pure Food and Drug Act allowed certain medicines to be sold by prescription only, and it required any habit-forming medicine to say so on the label. Many of the women who had taken patent medicine for their "female problems" didn't know that it contained morphine, or that morphine was addictive. The public education inspired by the Pure Food and Drug Act dramatically reduced addiction rates.

The criminalization of drugs had less utilitarian origins. It began in San Francisco, in 1875. Fear spread that Chinese men were using opium to seduce white women, and the city banned smoking it. It remained legal to possess opium as "laudanum," a drink mixed with alcohol, which was the main way that whites consumed it.

Cocaine starting getting a bad rap in the early 1900s, also because of racial concerns. Allegations spread that black cocaine "fiends" were raping white women or going on murderous sprees while they were high on the drug. The drug was reputed to give blacks superhuman powers. A *New York Times* article from 1914 is illustrative of the panic. It describes the Asheville, North Carolina, police chief's efforts to arrest a "hitherto inoffensive negro" who was now "running amuck in a cocaine frenzy."

> Knowing that he must kill this man or be killed himself, the Chief drew his revolver, placed the muzzle over the negro's heart, and fired — "intending to kill him right quick," as the officer tells but the shot did not even stagger the man. And a second shot that pierced the arm and entered the chest had as little effect in stopping his charge or checking his attack.
>
> Meanwhile, the Chief, out of the corner of his eye, saw infuriated negroes rushing toward the cabin from all direc-

tions. He had only three cartridges remaining in his gun, and he might need these in a minute to stop the mob. So he saved his ammunition and "finished the man with his club."

The following day, the Chief exchanged his revolver for one of heavier calibre. Yet, the one with which he shot the negro was a heavy, army model, using a cartridge that Lieutenant Townsend Whelen, who is an authority on such matters, recently declared was large enough to "kill any game in America." And many other officers in the South, who appreciate the increased vitality of the cocaine-crazed negroes, have made a similar exchange for guns of greater shocking power for the express purpose of combating the "fiend" when he runs amok.[1]

Marijuana prohibition was also tied to race. One of the arguments made on the floor of the Texas senate was "All Mexicans are crazy, and this stuff [marijuana] is what makes them crazy." In Montana the legislative history of marijuana criminalization reflects the following analysis: "Give one of these Mexican beet field workers a couple of puffs on a marijuana cigarette and he thinks he is in the bullring at Barcelona."[2]

Federal criminal laws soon followed: the Harrison Act in 1914 for opiates and cocaine, the Eighteenth Amendment, which banned the manufacture and sale of alcohol in 1919, and the Marijuana Tax Act in 1937.

THE "WAR" AND MASS INCARCERATION

The War on Drugs was launched in 1971 by President Richard Nixon. Declaring drugs "public enemy number one," Nixon was the only president to authorize more money for treatment than for punishment. Since the Nixon administration, the battle has been waged on the punishment front instead, including the provision of federal money to local police departments to make drug arrests.[3] Drug users and sellers, rather than drugs, have become the new public enemy. In 2006, 1,889,810 people were arrested for drug crimes, 829,625 people arrested for marijuana crimes alone.[4]

The War on Drugs is the single most important explanation for mass incarceration. Over 80 percent of the increase in the federal prison population from 1985 to 1995 was due to drug convictions.[5] Over the years 1925 to 1975, the United States incarcerated 110 people for every 100,000 in the population annually. Now the rate is 751.[6] As explained in the previous chapter, this has pushed us past the tipping point. The War on Drugs has created a rate of incarceration that makes us less safe.

This is an unsurprising result. Over 500,000 people are currently in prison in the United States for drug offenses.[7] One in five federal prisoners is a "low-level drug law violator," which means "non-violent offenders with minimal or no prior criminal history."[8] What the War on Drugs means is that we've taken nonviolent offenders, exposed them to violent ones, and then reintroduced them to our communities. A recent study notes the tragic result: "Department of Corrections data show that about a fourth of those initially imprisoned for nonviolent crimes are sentenced for a second time for committing a violent offense. Whatever else it reflects, this pattern highlights the possibility that prison serves to transmit violent habits and values rather than to reduce them."[9]

In addition to dramatically stepping up enforcement, lawmakers increased sentences. Now, on average, drug offenders serve longer federal sentences (seventy-eight months) than federal prisoners incarcerated for rape (sixty-seven months), burglary (fifty-one months), aggravated assault (fifty months), and auto theft (thirty-seven months).[10] Since 1989 more people have been incarcerated for drug offenses than for all violent offenses combined.[11]

A REPORT FROM THE FRONT:
OPERATION METH MERCHANT

"Operation Meth Merchant" was a joint investigation conducted in 2005 by the Federal Drug Enforcement Administration and state and local police agencies in Georgia. It was supposed to stop the selling of ingredients that can be used to manufacture methamphetamine, aka crystal meth. Northwest Georgia is a primary source of the highly addictive drug.

Police informants were sent into convenience stores. They bought things like cold medicine, cooking fuel, and matchbooks. They told the clerks at the stores that they needed the products "to cook." According to prosecutors, those words were sufficient to indicate to the clerks that the items would be used to make crystal meth. On those facts, forty-nine convenience store employees were charged with drug offenses — all for selling legal products like charcoal and Sudafed.

Twenty-three of the twenty-four stores that were investigated were owned by South Asians. Even though white people own 80 percent of the convenience stores in the area, and big retailers like Wal-Mart, Target, and CVS sell the same products, none of those stores were targeted.

The American Civil Liberties Union moved to dismiss the cases, alleging selective prosecution and noting that many of the people arrested barely spoke English, much less understood crystal meth slang. It presented sworn statements that informants had also told the police about sixteen white-owned convenience stores where they had purchased products to make meth, but that the police ignored those tips. The judge denied the motion.

The accused convenience store employees face up to twenty-five years in prison, fines up to $250,000, and forfeiture of their stores. Noncitizens convicted of crimes will be deported after they have served their prison sentences.

WHY PROHIBITION CAN'T WORK

Ending the War on Drugs is the best way to stop mass incarceration and make neighborhoods safer. It is hard to conceive of a public policy more at odds with both public welfare and basic
economics. When there is a product people want, someone will be
willing to supply it. Outlawing the product doesn't stop people
from getting it; it just creates an illegal market. The illegal market
drives up the cost, which means high profits for the marketeers. Violence becomes one of the ways competitors are eliminated. Thus
the violence associated with drugs is better understood as a consequence of the illegal market created by the criminalization of the
drug trade. At the end of this chapter, and in chapter 8, I suggest
better ways to prevent drug abuse.

During the United States' first experiment with Prohibition,
when it was a crime to sell alcohol, Al Capone made $60 million a
year from alcohol sales. Naturally the big bucks attracted some
competitors. Nowadays we would call Big Al's method of resolving disputes "drive-by shootings." Maybe you've seen the movie
montages: the Chicago river running red with all the spilled
blood.

The only thing that stopped the violence was the Eighteenth
Amendment to the United States Constitution. Repealing Prohibition, it declared the War on Liquor over. Liquor won.

Prohibition's end had been hastened by a letter in the *New York
Times*, written by John D. Rockefeller to Nicholas Murray Butler,
president of Columbia University, in 1932. It was published on the
front page:

> When [Prohibition was introduced] I earnestly hoped that
> it would be generally supported by the public opinion. This
> has not been the result, but rather drinking generally has
> increased; the speakeasy has replaced the saloon; a vast army

of lawbreakers has been recruited and financed on a colossal scale; many of our best citizens have openly and unabashedly disregarded the Eighteenth Amendment; respect for all law has greatly lessened; and crime has increased to an unprecedented degree.[12]

One of today's billionaires could write the same letter, substituting "drugs" for "alcohol."

With intoxicating substances, including the nicotine in tobacco, we have two — and only two — basic choices. Neither is perfect; it's just a matter of choosing the one with the more acceptable downside:

> *Choice 1:* We can accept that people are going to obtain these substances, and reduce the harm as best we can.
>
> *Choice 2:* We can pretend that we can stop people from using these substances, and punish them for what they put into their bodies.

When we choose to punish, the result is as Rockefeller described: an increase in users, a vast army of lawbreakers, open disrespect for the law, and a rise in crime.

THE WAR'S LEGACY

- Twice as many people die from using drugs now as died from drug use before the War on Drugs.[13]
- Forty-five percent of Americans have used illegal drugs at some point in their lifetimes. Fifteen percent have used illegal drugs within the last year.[14]
- Eighty-five percent of high school seniors said, in 2006, that marijuana is "fairly easy" or "very easy" to get.[15]
- Revenues would rank the illegal drug business number 13 on the Fortune 500 list of largest U.S. corporations.[16]

- Mild versions of drugs (coca leaves, for example, rather than powdered cocaine) are consumed in their countries of origin. The most dangerous and potent forms of drugs are exported to the United States.[17]

THE COST TO FREEDOM

Drugs are the subject of most of the cases in which the Supreme Court has expanded police power. Here's the problem: drugs are illegal, and they are easy to hide; for police to find them, they have to look hard, which often means they invade the privacy of innocent people.

In recent years, using drugs as the rationale, federal courts have ruled that it is constitutional for police dogs to sniff the luggage of everyone at the airport,[18] for the police to detain people for trivial offenses when their real motive is to look for drugs,[19] for police to get people to "consent" to searches without knowing they have the right to say "no,"[20] for school districts to require high school students to take drug tests in order to participate in extracurricular activities,[21] and for authorities to profile people based on their race—all in the service of the War on Drugs.

The problem is even worse in state courts, where 90 percent of drug prosecutions occur. Not wanting to appear "soft on crime," judges may be tempted to admit evidence even when police have crossed the line. Since 90 percent of people charged with crimes plead guilty—often to avoid severe mandatory sentences if they go to trial and lose—the judge's decision in a "plea bargain" usually is not subject to review (in most states when you plead guilty, you give up your right to appeal).

As an example of the extraordinary power the War on Drugs gives to police, consider how accommodating courts have been in allowing cops to detain people to investigate them for drug crimes. In various cases, courts have ruled that the following behavior is "suspicious" enough to support a police investigation for carrying drugs on an airplane:

Arriving late at night
Arriving early in the morning

One of first to deplane
One of last to deplane
Deplaning in the middle

Using a one-way ticket
Using a round-trip ticket

Carrying brand-new luggage
Carrying a small gym bag

Traveling alone
Traveling with a companion

Acting too nervous
Acting too calm

Wearing expensive clothing and gold jewelry
Dressing in black corduroys, white pullover shirt, loafers
    without socks
Dressing in dark slacks, work shirt, hat
Dressing in brown leather aviator jacket, gold chain, hair
    down to shoulders
Dressing in loose-fitting sweatshirt, denim jacket

Walking rapidly through airport
Walking aimlessly through airport

Flying into Washington National Airport on the LaGuardia
    Shuttle
Carrying a white handkerchief in his hand[22]

THE BETTER CHOICE

> Harm reduction is the conviction that people should not be punished
> for what they put into their bodies, but only for crimes committed
> against others. It acknowledges that no society will ever be free of
> drugs. It holds that drug policies should seek to reduce the negative
> consequences of both drug use and the policies themselves.
>
> —Drug Policy Alliance

- Approximately half of property crime, robberies, and burglaries are the result of the high cost of drugs that is a direct result of the War on Drugs.[23]
- A study showed that a group of 150 drug addicts committed 96 percent fewer crimes when they had access to a lower-cost drug supply.[24]
- Every dollar invested in substance abuse treatment saves taxpayers $7.46 in other costs.[25]

If the War on Drugs has been a failure, then what? We don't have to throw in the towel on solving the problems caused by drugs, and we don't have to go the route to complete legalization. There is a better way.

If you think that designated drivers are a good idea when people are going out for a night on the town, you are already a fan of the public health policy known as "harm reduction." This philosophy accepts that people will engage in certain kinds of risky conduct, and seeks to minimize the danger. In the language of hip-hop, harm reduction "keeps it real."

Harm reduction is a proven successful strategy for dealing with the risks posed by drugs. One of its most prominent achievements has been needle-exchange programs, which are credited with dramatic reductions in HIV transmission among drug injectors.[26]

The goal of drug harm reduction is to mitigate the harm that some drug users do to themselves and others. It also seeks to reverse the bad consequences of drug use, including the violence-prone illegal drug market. It acknowledges that some drugs are worse than others, and that there are safer and less safe ways of using drugs.

Three Components of a U.S. Harm Reduction Program

- Possession of small amounts of drugs for personal use should be decriminalized.
- Treatment programs should be available for every addict.
- Needle-exchange and drug testing services should be made available to reduce the risks of disease transmission and overdose.

These measures are already widely practiced around the world, including in the Netherlands, France, Spain, Italy, and Mexico. Harm reduction has also been instituted in some U.S. cities, including San Francisco, where the possession of small amounts of marijuana is not prosecuted, and where needle-exchange programs are promoted by the government.[27]

Harm reduction has several advantages over a strategy of punishment. The most important is public safety. It reduces the size of the illegal market for drugs, making them less expensive. With cheaper drugs, addicts would commit fewer crimes (there are millions more alcoholics in the U.S. than heroin junkies, but because alcohol is relatively cheap, there is not a serious problem with alcoholics stealing to support their drinking).

The other public safety benefit of harm reduction is that it reduces the violence associated with the illegal drug market. Just as Al Capone and his ilk disappeared when Prohibition was repealed, so too will the violent warfare between the profiteers, once the high profits of an unregulated market leave the drug trade. Budweiser and Heineken battle with cute commercials during the Super Bowl, not drive-by shootings.

Harm reduction recognizes that since there has never, in the history of the world, been a drug-free society, we benefit more from making drugs safer than from pretending that we can eradicate them. DanceSafe, a nonprofit organization operating in twenty-eight states, is an example of this approach. It offers drug-testing services at nightclubs and parties where Ecstasy and other illegal drugs are likely to be consumed. Allowing users to know exactly what is in the substances they are consuming would also be a boon for public health. We know how much alcohol is in our beer and vodka, and how much acetaminophen is in our Tylenol. Knowing whether a pill purported to be Ecstasy contains only the relatively mild MDMA or instead is adulterated with some more dangerous substance, like PCP or LSD, could save lives.[28]

We don't know why most people who use illegal drugs are able to do so recreationally but a few others become addicted to them. What is clear, however, is that the threat of punishment does not encourage addicts to seek the treatment that they need. The harm reduction approach is consistent with what the National Institutes of Health (NIH) says about addicts: they are sick, not immoral. The NIH Web site states:

> Drug addiction is a complex but treatable disease. . . . For many people, drug abuse becomes chronic, with relapses possible even after long periods of abstinence. In fact, relapse to drug abuse occurs at rates similar to those for other well-characterized, chronic medical illnesses such as diabetes, hypertension, and asthma. As a chronic, recurring illness, addiction may require repeated episodes of treatment before sustained abstinence is achieved.[29]

In approaching the care of addicts with the same dignity as we approach the care of other sick people, harm reduction is a more scientific, more compassionate alternative to incarceration.

Some people worry that harm reduction sends the message that drugs are okay, which might encourage their use. In countries in which drugs have been decriminalized, however, usage has not increased. Indeed, when marijuana became legally available in the

Netherlands, its usage actually decreased.[30]

Harm reduction would also make prevention efforts for more addictive drugs like meth, cocaine, and heroin more credible. There are already examples of public education campaigns reducing the demand for truly dangerous drugs. Campaigns targeting crystal meth use in the gay community, for example, are showing signs of success.

But the best example of the success of a public health campaign to stop use of a dangerous drug is the one targeting tobacco. Nicotine is probably the most addictive of all drugs, and, along with alcohol, has caused the greatest economic losses, especially in terms of health care.[31] Rather than lock up cigarette users, the United States has educated them about the dangers of the drug. It is the one area of drug policy about which the United States can brag and tout some success. Tobacco use among the young is lower than in many other countries around the world.[32] It's a compelling example of the virtue of public education and health care rather than punishment.

Full-scale legalization would not have to occur to achieve the benefits of harm reduction. In many nations in Western Europe drugs are still criminalized, but enforcement is more strategic than in the United States. We can reduce some of the draconian mandatory minimum sentences for drug crimes, for example, while still retaining the criminal justice system as one tool. Prosecutions simply should not be the only tool or the primary means of addressing the drug issue.

To acknowledge that there is no easy answer to the problems presented by drugs is not to say that the status quo is acceptable. The day that we bring the troops—the police and the prosecutors— home from the War on Drugs, the United States will be a safer, and more free, country.

4

Jury Duty: Power to the People

While I earned my living by putting people in prison, I discovered a secret power in our criminal justice system. It changed my life, and could help remedy the problem of mass incarceration. My guides were the jurors of the District of Columbia. These citizens showed up for jury duty but stayed to do justice. Some people might call their actions radical, but they have much to teach us all. They demonstrate how "We the People" can take back American criminal justice—to make us all safe and free.

OPENING ARGUMENT

"Good afternoon, ladies and gentlemen of the jury. My name is Paul Butler and I represent the United States of America."

That's how I always started my opening statement. Most of the jurors were black like me. They were usually old folks—the main group who bothered to show up for jury duty in career-obsessed DC. As they arrived at the courthouse in their Sunday go-to-church clothes, they seemed not so far removed from the time when their families migrated to DC from North Carolina in the 1950s. Sure, it was a bother to be called to jury duty, but it was also a privilege—they could remember when no black person ever received a jury summons. And then to actually be selected for a jury! They had figured the defendant was going to be black, and they were right. But what they hadn't expected was this other African American man in the courtroom.

There I was in a suit and tie, representing the United States. My presence reminded these jurors of the civil rights movement, the journey from slavery to freedom, and the promise of America — what I, tall and proud, brought to their minds as I paced the well of the courtroom. These old black people would beam at me like they were thinking, *You go boy! You represent the United States of America!*

"ANOTHER BLACK MAN TO JAIL"

Here's the thing. The comfort my presence was intended to provide worked some of the time, but not all of the time. During training, we rookie prosecutors were warned that there would be times that we would persuade a jury that the defendant was guilty but the jury would still find him "not guilty." They would do this because "they didn't want to send another black man to jail."

The most famous example of a DC jury refusing to convict an obviously guilty person involves Marion Barry, the former mayor. During the 1980s, Barry was so popular among African American voters that one local newspaper dubbed him "mayor for life." Many white folks, on the other hand, couldn't stand him — he was arrogant and unpolished, and there were consistent rumors that he was corrupt and/or on drugs.

In 1990 the FBI persuaded Rasheeda Moore, the mayor's old paramour, to set him up. She telephoned him, said that she was in town for a short time, and invited him to her hotel room. Barry arrived at the lobby and tried to persuade her to come downstairs for a drink. She insisted that he come to her room instead. After he did, they talked for a while and Moore then produced crack cocaine and a pipe. Barry first said he didn't want to smoke it, but later consented. As soon as he inhaled, FBI and Metropolitan Police agents stormed the room and arrested the mayor. The videotape of the mayor smoking crack became the key evidence in the trial.

In the nation's capital, the case caused a huge racial firestorm. Barry's defense team fanned the flames by asserting he was the victim of a racist prosecution. At that time I worked in the U.S. Attorney's Office that was prosecuting Barry.

To my surprise some of my fellow African American prosecutors hoped that the mayor would be acquitted. Since law enforcement officers in the District of Columbia hear many rumors about prominent officials, many of them white, engaging in illegal conduct, including drug use, some black prosecutors wondered why, of all those people, the government chose to set up the most famous black politician in the city. (They also asked why, if crack is so dangerous, the FBI had allowed the mayor to smoke it.) The predominantly black jury must have had similar concerns: it failed to convict the mayor of possession of cocaine, even though the jurors saw him smoking it on the FBI videotape.

We rookie prosecutors were warned we would see juries do this often in drug cases and rarely in cases involving violent crime. The experienced prosecutors—mainly white guys—communicated this with an air of exasperation. They would often mutter something about DC juries. Here they were in the prosecutor's office trying to help these poor black folks, and these juries didn't have the good sense to lock up all of their . . . cretins.

They were right. We rookies mainly respected the jurors, but sometimes they would disgust us. We knew the cretin was guilty, they knew he was guilty, yet sometimes, if it was a drug case, they would refuse to convict.

I prosecuted a case in which the dope boy was a nineteen-year-old with a baby face. On the witness stand he admitted that when the police arrested him they found a glassine envelope containing cocaine in his pocket. The kid claimed he didn't know how it got there. The defense produced no other witnesses. Open-and-shut case for the prosecution, I thought, so when the foreperson announced "not guilty," I couldn't believe it. After the jurors were dismissed, I followed them out of the courtroom. None of the blacks would talk to me, but the lone white juror—a middle-aged woman—stopped. "We knew he was guilty," she said, "but he was so young."

In general I had the highest respect for jurors, but when they did stuff like this, I thought they were crazy. When I left the prosecutor's office and became a professor, I wanted to study this phenomenon immediately. Why would a juror vote to let a guilty person go free? Assuming that the juror is a sensible person, she must believe that she and her community are, in some way, better off with the defendant out of prison than in prison. But how could any rational person believe that about a criminal?

I came to understand that what these old black people were doing was in the highest service of justice. When these jurors refused to convict people they knew were guilty, they were walking up to a world that called people like their grandchildren "cretins" and slapping that world in the face.

Imagine a country that has statistics like DC's in which more than one-third of the young male citizens are under the supervision of the criminal justice system: they either are in prison, on probation or parole, or have a trial coming up. Imagine a country in which two-thirds of the young men can anticipate being arrested before they reach age thirty. Imagine a country in which there are more young men in prison than in college. Now give the citizens of the country the key to the jail. Should they use it?

Such a country sounds like a police state. When we criticize those kinds of regimes, we think that the problem lies not with the citizens of the state, but rather with the government or law. This is what DC jurors were saying when they emancipated black men guilty of nonviolent crimes (there was rarely nullification in crimes with victims; jurors voted "not guilty" in those cases because they had reasonable doubt about the government's evidence, often because they didn't believe the police). The defendants in the drug cases reminded them of people they knew: the kid in the neighborhood who was up to no good hanging out on the corner, but who also helped the old lady next door take her groceries up four flights of stairs, or the quiet young man who drove his grandfather to kidney dialysis twice a week. And they could remember when he was ten years old and so excited because his daddy was going to pick him up and he waited on the porch, and waited, and his father never came. And they knew his mother tried to get him to stay in school . . . but kids are hardheaded.

When these jurors looked at this other young man in chains, all these memories came back. Those memories seemed relevant to the case, regardless of what the law said. The law responded to these problems by locking that man in a cage. But for once these jurors had some power over the law, and when they got a little power they used it the best way they knew how.

JURY NULLIFICATION: A PRIMER

When a jury disregards the evidence and acquits an otherwise guilty defendant, it has practiced jury nullification. The jury is saying that the law is unfair, either generally or in this particular case. The jury's decision is totally legal — indeed, the practice of jury nullification is a proud part of U.S. constitutional history.

The Constitution was written by men who were very suspicious of the power of government. Prosecutors were viewed as a necessary evil, but the framers didn't trust them much. Thus the right to trial by jury was guaranteed in the Bill of Rights.

This right was an important component of democracy in the new country. People from the community — not the government — would have the final say in whether a person would be punished. Jurors were supposed to be an important limit on government power — part of the complex system of checks and balances that was designed to prevent the state from becoming too overbearing.

A THOUGHT EXPERIMENT

It is 1853, and you are a juror in a criminal case in Boston. The defendant has been accused of breaking the law by helping a slave escape to freedom in Canada. You are persuaded that the prosecutors have proved beyond a reasonable doubt that the defendant is guilty of helping free the slave. Will you vote to convict?

If you vote "not guilty," you have engaged in jury nullification. Jurors nullify most frequently when they think the law is unjust or the prosecution is unfair. During the shameful time in American history when slavery was legal, many jurors acquitted people guilty of helping slaves escape. This was jury nullification's finest hour.

But it was as controversial then as it is now. Were these jurors heroes because they used the power they had to subvert an immoral law? They must have believed that the need to protest the evil of slavery trumped their obligation to follow the judge's instructions and even their oath to consider the evidence in the case objectively.

Some people would say, however, that in addition to subverting an immoral law, the activist jurors also subverted democracy. People who aided runaway slaves were prosecuted under the Fugitive Slave Act. This act, passed by Congress in 1850, was affirmed by the Supreme Court in its infamous decision in the *Dred Scott* case. Maybe the jurors who were against slavery should have tried to persuade Congress to repeal the act rather than take the law into their own hands.

Since leaving the prosecutor's office, I have become a scholar of jury nullification, and in the last ten years I have discussed the fugitive slave cases with hundreds of people. Most say that the abolitionist jurors acted properly. These people proclaim that if they had been jurors in those cases, they too would have set the guilty defendants free. A substantial minority of people I've spoken to— none of whom supports slavery—believes that the jurors should have convicted, regardless of their feelings about the law.

For my own answer, I call upon two parts of my life experience. As a prosecutor in the Department of Justice, my specialty was going after corrupt public officials. I used the law as a weapon against those who were supposed to make or enforce it but who had instead abused it. The touchstone, then, of my briefs and oral arguments was that no person should be above the law. But I am also the descendant of slaves. Nobody knows as well as my people that God does not make the laws of the United States; imperfect human beings do, and at times they have made laws that are extraordinarily unjust—even beneath respect. These experiences lead me to admire the jurors in the fugitive slave cases who set aside the law to follow their own vision of justice. They were correct to subvert prosecutions that were fundamentally unfair.

I think that nullification is an appropriate response to overzealous prosecutors even today. I understand the concerns, I see the slippery slope. At the end of the day, however, my experiences as a prosecutor grant me confidence in the wisdom of nullification in appropriate cases.

As a prosecutor I had some say about which cases to bring to trial. I did not always prosecute people I thought were guilty.[1] That wasn't nullification; it was "prosecutorial discretion." Before cases came to me, law enforcement officers—police and FBI agents—often decided not to arrest people they knew were guilty.

Maybe a cop thought a dime bag of marijuana wasn't worth saddling a kid with a criminal record. Perhaps an FBI agent thought a charge against a popular official right before an election would be seen as political, or be so divisive that it would do more harm than good. Such extrajudicial acts of excusing criminal conduct seldom upset most people. Ironically, it is only when a jury does it, as opposed to one police officer or one prosecutor, that a hue and cry ensues.

My experience as a prosecutor also instilled in me a profound respect for another integral part of American criminal justice: the right to trial by jury. The framers of the Constitution may have stained the document with their toleration of slavery, but trial by

jury is one thing that they got very right. I developed an almost re-
ligious faith in the ability of twelve people drawn from the community to reach a proper verdict. Most times, when twelve of them
agree on a verdict—even a verdict that represents nullification—
citizens should be satisfied that justice has been done.

SUSPICION OF THE PEOPLE

It seems now that many American courts would prefer to reserve
doing justice for the "experts"—presumably the politicians and
government bureaucrats who got us into this mass incarceration
mess in the first place. They envision the juror's proper role as that
of a kind of scientist who objectively determines facts. They really
don't trust their fellow citizens much; one imagines they might
welcome a technology that would replace human jurors with ro-
botic ones. Microchip-encoded robots, after all, could do better
forensic analysis than twelve citizens randomly pulled off the
street.

Evidence of the wariness with which some judges regard nullification can be seen in *United States v. Thomas*, a case decided in
New York in 1997.[2] Ten African Americans were accused of selling
cocaine. All of the jurors were white except for one black man.
The prosecution had tried to eliminate the African American from
the jury pool, but the judge wouldn't allow it because he didn't
want an all-white jury. During the trial, six jurors complained to
the judge that the black juror was distracting them by squeaking
his shoe against the floor, rustling cough drop wrappers in his
pocket, and agreeing with points that the defense made by slapping his leg and saying "yes" and "yeah."

The judge stopped the trial and questioned the jurors about
whether the black man was disturbing them so much they
couldn't render a fair verdict. All the jurors thought that they could
proceed. During their deliberations, however, some white jurors
again complained that the black juror was refusing to consider
voting guilty because he did not want to convict "his people" or

because he thought the defendants were dealing drugs out of economic necessity.

The judge then called another hearing, in which some of the jurors claimed the African American juror was nullifying, but others said he just didn't think the evidence was strong enough in the case. The judge kicked the black man off the jury because, the judge said, he had "preconceived, fixed, cultural, economic, or social . . . reasons that are totally improper and impermissible." The eleven white jurors went on to convict all but one of the defendants.

The defense then appealed the conviction. The Court of Appeals ruled that the trial judge should not have excluded the African American juror. The appellate court was critical of nullification but said there wasn't enough evidence that the black juror was going to nullify for him to have been dismissed.

Judges are forbidden from intruding on juror deliberations unless there is overwhelming evidence of misconduct. If judges have extremely clear proof, they can try to stop nullification before the verdict is rendered (on the ground that the juror is not "impartially" considering the evidence in the case). After the verdict, however, there is nothing they can do, regardless of their personal preferences. The power to nullify is protected by the United States Constitution. Pursuant to the Eighth Amendment's double jeopardy clause, no judge can reverse a jury verdict of "not guilty" — even when the judge disagrees with the jury, or when the acquittal is not supported by evidence. That's why even if O.J. Simpson confessed to murder, which he seems to have come close to doing in the book *If I Did It*, he cannot be put on trial again.

Not all judges disapprove of nullification. After law school I clerked for Mary Johnson Lowe, a federal judge in New York. When she instructed jurors on the burden of proof, she would say, "If you find guilt beyond a reasonable doubt, you *may* convict." Sometimes the prosecution would object and ask the judge to say "*must* convict." The judge had been a defense attorney in the Bronx, and she didn't have much confidence in the New York

Police Department when it came to minority suspects. "Objection overruled," she'd say, slamming down the gavel.

Jury nullification works only in one direction—in favor of "not guilty" verdicts. If a jury wrongly convicts someone, the Constitution allows judges to overturn that verdict (as opposed to a not-guilty verdict) if it is unsupported by evidence. The framers wanted to give more leeway to juries to acquit than to convict. They trusted citizens more, and prosecutors less.

A BRIEF HISTORY

The idea of giving ordinary citizens the power to thwart prosecutions was attractive to early Americans because of their experience with the English loyalists. The Crown's rebellious subjects in the colonies were constantly being charged with crimes. The problem for the prosecution was that these defendants had the right to a trial by a jury of their peers—their proudly American, anti-British peers.

In one famous case, John Peter Zenger, the American revolutionary, was accused of "seditious libel" because he had published statements critical of English rule. For this crime, it was the judge who was supposed to decide whether the statements made by the defendant were libelous. (The jury's job was to decide if the defendant actually made the statements.) The judge in Zenger's case found that the statements were libelous, as a matter of law.

Then history was made. Zenger's defense attorney gave a closing statement in which he told the jury to ignore what the judge had said. The jury, he proclaimed, had the power to decide the law for itself. The jury, famously, acquitted Zenger. This case came to symbolize the power of the people, through the jury trial system, to defeat the government when it acts like a tyrant.

Some people who don't like jury nullification predict a doomsday scenario if it is widely practiced. An analysis of American history suggests that this concern is misplaced. After Zenger's trial, the idea that juries should decide "justice" became settled in

American jurisprudence. Almost every court endorsed this principle; juries were even instructed on their power to decide the law as well as the facts. There is no evidence that juries nullified all the time simply because they could; it was a power that they used sparingly, perhaps because prosecutors were careful about the cases that they brought, knowing that jurors could check their power if they thought law enforcement was getting out of hand.

The point here is that jurors could emancipate some guilty criminals and the system still worked—the sun and the moon did not fall out of the sky. Indeed, the jury system seems to have worked quite well. It wasn't until the late 1800s, when the industrial revolution took full effect in the United States, that the prerogative of jurors to decide the law was called into question.

At this time big business became a political force, and the rich guys wanted the law to be very settled, predictable, and probusiness, which meant taking power out of the hands of the people. Finally, in a 1895 case called *Sparf v. United States*, the United States Supreme Court dealt a blow to jury nullification.

THE SECRET POWER

In *Sparf*, the Supreme Court acknowledged that juries have the "physical power" to disregard the law, but stated that they have no "moral right" to do so. Indeed, the Court observed, "If the jury were at liberty to settle the law for themselves, the effect would be . . . that the law itself would be most uncertain, from the different views, which different juries might take of it." It seems that the newly powerful corporations were just a little scared of individual citizens. They preferred that the state, rather than the jury, determine what was fair.

Despite the Supreme Court's critique of nullification, the Court conceded that it could not stop jurors from nullifying; the only way that could happen would be by taking the right to trial by jury out of the Bill of Rights. The Court, however, tried to discourage nullification by creating a bizarre double standard: jurors may have the ability to nullify, the Court held, but they shouldn't be told they have it. So nullification has become a secret power of jurors. When they do it, they act lawfully, but no one is required to tell them beforehand that they have this option.

Since *Sparf*, most of the appellate courts that have considered jury nullification have addressed this bizarre anomaly and have endorsed it. But not every court has been critical of nullification. In 1972, the United States Court of Appeals for the District of Columbia approved of limited nullification "as a necessary counter to case-hardened judges and arbitrary prosecutors." The DC circuit court was concerned, however, that "what makes for health as an occasional medicine would be disastrous as a daily diet."

In addition to the fugitive slave cases, jury nullification is credited for not-guilty verdicts in cases involving prosecutions of Prohibition-era alcohol crimes, anti–Vietnam War protestors, and gay sex between consenting adults (before the Supreme Court decision in 2003 declaring such prosecutions unconstitutional). Not all cases of nullification are heralded, though, even by its proponents. During the civil rights movement some people accused of violence against civil rights activists were acquitted in the face of substantial evidence of their guilt. If the fugitive slave cases were nullification at its best, these cases were nullification at its worst. The lesson is that nullification is like any other powerful tool: depending upon whose hands it is in, it can be used for good or for evil.

NULLIFICATION TODAY

The law regarding nullification has not changed much since *Sparf* was decided in 1895. In the federal system and in most of the states, jurors are not instructed on their power to judge the law. Under the constitutions of four states (Indiana, Georgia, Maryland, and Oregon),[3] however, jurors are explicitly given the power to "judge" the criminal law.[4] Twenty-five states have considered legislation that would obligate the judge to instruct the jury about its right to nullify. In 2002, for example, South Dakota voters rejected a proposal to amend the state constitution to permit criminal defendants to make defenses based on nullification.

Lower courts generally have followed the Supreme Court's lead in *Sparf* in discouraging nullification.[5] But they have set the standards high for determining when trial judges can remove jurors who are suspected of being potential nullifiers. In the *United States v. Thomas* case discussed earlier in this chapter, the appellate court reversed the trial judge's decision to remove a juror. The court held that a juror can be removed on suspicion of nullification only when there is no possibility that the juror's analysis is based on the evidence in the case. The appellate court also warned trial judges against intrusive examination of individual jurors about the substance of their deliberations.

Similarly, a Colorado appellate court dismissed the prosecution of a juror who was believed to have favored nullification.[6] Laura Kriho was the lone holdout in a drug possession case, which caused the jury to hang. During jury selection, Kriho did not disclose her own arrest for a drug crime or her membership in organizations trying to legalize marijuana. After the trial, she was prosecuted for contempt of court. The appellate court, in dismissing the prosecution, criticized jury nullification, but it established principles offering more protection to jurors who covertly nullify than to the prosecutors who would thwart them. Basically, unless a juror openly admits that she is nullifying, she cannot be removed from the jury.

The political debate about nullification focuses on how often it occurs and whether it should be encouraged or discouraged. As with most aspects of the jury deliberation process, there is scant empirical data. Jurors rarely admit that they have nullified. Perhaps this means that nullification does not happen frequently. It may also be the case that jurors are reluctant to admit nullifying because they are uncertain whether they have acted legally. For example, the jurors who refused to convict Marion Barry of cocaine possession later said that they believed that Barry had been the victim of entrapment and selective prosecution. None openly acknowledged that they nullified the drug possession charge.

Although the empirical evidence on nullification is slim, anecdotal evidence abounds. Whenever there is a not-guilty verdict in a high-profile case, nullification is frequently suspected. Prime examples include the so-called Rodney King case (King was the victim, not the defendant), in which two white police officers were found not guilty of the brutal beating, captured on video, of an African American man, and the O.J. Simpson case, in which jurors declined to convict Simpson of murder. The jurors in both cases denied that they had nullified. In the Simpson case, some of the jurors said they thought the government had proven only that Simpson was "probably" guilty but had not satisfied the burden of proof beyond a reasonable doubt.[7]

Some lawyers have wondered whether black jurors, motivated by racial concerns about the criminal justice system, are more likely to acquit black defendants. This is frequently expressed as a concern about not wanting to "send another black man to prison." I wrote an article in the *Yale Law Journal* suggesting that African American jurors conduct a kind of cost-benefit analysis.[8] I believe that nullification occurs with some frequency in low-level drug cases, but almost never in cases of violent crime. In the drug cases, the jurors are protesting selective prosecution of young black men, and especially the "War on Drugs." In the article, I wrote that black jurors act morally when they use their power to protest this kind of discrimination. I endorse this kind of nullification when it is selective and careful (for example, nullification would be inappropriate when dealers sell drugs to minors) because discriminatory prosecutions have resulted in the mass incarceration of young African American men.

I understand that this point of view is controversial. I am inspired, however, by the churchgoing, often elderly Americans whom I observed engaging in this nullification at the District of Columbia Superior Court. I don't think these people would describe themselves as radical or as legal activists. They might say, instead, that for once in their lives they had a little power and they used it to help remedy an overbearing government. If the framers of the Constitution could remove their racial blinders, I think they would be proud.

IS NULLIFICATION ANTIDEMOCRATIC?

What about the concern that nullification is inconsistent with the rule of law? In an important article, Professor Darryl Brown investigated this claim.[9] He divided jurors' rationales for nullification into four categories:

- They believe the law is unjust.
- They believe an otherwise fair law is being unfairly applied in a particular case.
- They are troubled by prosecutorial misconduct.
- They are biased in favor of the accused person or against the prosecutor.

Professor Brown asserts that only the last category contravenes the rule of law. Fortunately, it also seems to be the most infrequent animus of nullification. I don't think this fact surprises most lawyers who have practiced in front of juries. There is something about the jury system that seems to inspire the best in citizens. This doesn't mean that jurors are free of prejudice. I do believe, however, that the jury selection process works to ferret out the kinds of racist jurors who gave nullification a bad name during the civil rights era.

The average citizen does not know much about nullification. It has a subversive, shadowy reputation that it does not deserve. It would be useful, however, to educate the public about nullification's important role in our constitutional history. The jurors in the eighteenth-century Zenger case were as integral to the formation of the democracy as the more radical protesters of the Boston Tea Party. Learning about the Zenger jurors will breed more, not less, respect for the jury system.

In a sense, the debate about nullification is a litmus test of how much people trust jurors. If, as many lawyers do, you trust them a great deal, you are not likely to be worried about jurors nullifying inappropriately. If, on the other hand, you don't put much faith in jurors to begin with, the prospect of nullification seems apocalyptic. Nullification is a limited remedy. It is also an essential component of the jury trial system, and from it we have nothing to fear.

MARTIN LUTHER KING JURORS

At this point every American citizen should ask whether he or she is satisfied to live in a country that has the highest rate of incarceration in the world. If not, there is something that you can do to help make the United States more safe and free.

Strategic jury nullification can safely reduce mass incarceration. The DC jurors were right: there are too many black men in prison. But they didn't go far enough. There are too many people in prison—period; too many men and too many women, of every race and ethnicity. A careful campaign of strategic nullification can help responsibly free those people for whom prison will do no good, and it can send a powerful message for change.

During the civil rights era, Martin Luther King Jr. was forced to resort to extreme tactics, which he called creative disobedience, to break down the walls of discrimination. With our criminal justice system hell-bent on locking up so many people for nonviolent conduct, now is the time for Martin Luther King jurors.

A PROPOSAL FOR STRATEGIC NULLIFICATION

- In cases involving the possession or sale of small amounts of drugs, every juror should consider voting not guilty, regardless of the evidence in the case.
- When a defendant is accused of murder, rape, robbery, theft, public corruption, corporate fraud, any other crime of vio-

lence, or any crime that has a victim, Martin Luther King jurors should *convict* if they are persuaded that the evidence proves the defendant guilty beyond a reasonable doubt.

- When a defendant is accused of selling drugs to minors, or providing drugs to anyone without their consent, Martin Luther King jurors should *convict* if there is proof beyond a reasonable doubt.
- When a defendant is accused of possessing drugs for his or her own use, or selling a small quantity of drugs to another consenting adult, Martin Luther King jurors should vote *"not guilty."*

This strategic nullification is perfectly legal, and has two great benefits. First, it helps the community by safely reducing the number of incarcerated people. Second, it sends the message that "We the People" want fundamental change in our criminal justice system. This message is intended for both lawmakers and prosecutors.

SAFER NEIGHBORHOODS

As we have seen, the United States has passed the tipping point for incarceration, and, as a result, we are less safe. There is an important correlation between incarceration and crime: in states where prison populations have been reduced, crime has subsequently fallen. If strategic nullification is effectively implemented, violent crime ultimately could decrease.

The DC jurors had it absolutely right: keeping people out of prison for nonviolent drug crimes is in the best interest of families and communities.

A public health and harm reduction approach to drugs would be more effective. Our vision for the future is treatment, not punishment. Safety, not locking people up, must be the object of our justice system.

DIRECT ACTION—INSIDE AND OUTSIDE
THE COURTROOM

Strategic nullification sends an important message to the powers that be. Like the civil rights activists who (illegally) sat in at lunch counters, Martin Luther King jurors who legally nullify say, "We are fed up and we're not going to take it anymore."

Nullification is the new-school form of civil disobedience. American history—from the end of slavery to the end of Jim Crow—teaches us that direct action is one of the best ways to achieve progress for people who have been discriminated against or shut out. It works when the traditional methods of petitioning lawmakers fail, as they do now with the dysfunctional politics of criminal justice.

Of course, the civil rights protestors didn't just stay at the lunch counters. They developed a vision for a better future, and they worked hard to achieve it. So too must our Martin Luther King jurors. Accordingly, any person who uses strategic nullification inside the courtroom must engage in outside-the-courtroom interventions as well. They would be obligated to take some civic intervention in the name of public safety and criminal justice.

The citizenship act should be some project that advances safety and justice—tutoring a child, teaching parenting skills to young adults, volunteering at a rape-crisis center, or mentoring a recently released inmate. The final chapter of *Let's Get Free* suggests seven ways that citizens can work for the change that our criminal justice system needs.

The DC jurors who taught me about nullification would admit that it is far from a perfect strategy. It's more a cry for help than a "solution" to all of the problems caused by mass incarceration and expanding police power. But since some citizens, especially in urban areas, are already choosing to nullify, a thoughtful and organized strategy would produce the best results. *Let's Get Free*'s proposal for responsible nullification is a powerful tool in an arsenal for change.

TEN QUESTIONS AND ANSWERS ABOUT STRATEGIC NULLIFICATION

1. Since most defendants plea-bargain, and only a few go to trial, how would nullification help?

Many defendants now plead guilty to receive a reduction in their sentence. They are concerned that if they go to trial and are convicted, the judge will throw the book at them. If defendants in nonviolent drug cases knew there was a possibility that he or she could have a MLK juror, they would be more willing to go to trial. According to some anecdotal evidence in jurisdictions where nullification occurs, relatively more defendants go to trial in drug cases.

2. Aren't juries in criminal cases required to be unanimous?

Yes. As a practical matter, just one MLK juror could force a hung jury, which would prevent a conviction. This is not technically jury nullification; the prosecutor could always bring the charges again since there has not been a unanimous verdict. In low-level drug cases, however, prosecutors often do not prosecute the case again when there is a hung jury.

3. Could MLK jurors be excluded from juries?

Prosecutors would undoubtedly try. Potential jurors would have to decide how "out" they wanted to be about their interest in strategic nullification. If they openly admitted it, they would probably be excluded from the jury. A similar issue arises with death penalty cases. The Supreme Court has ruled that people who are opposed to the death penalty can be barred from sitting on those juries. Abolitionist lawyers and the civil rights and faith communities have responded in two ways. First, they have advised potential jurors to be thoughtful about how they answer questions during the jury selection process. For example, potential jurors are instructed to say they are not opposed to the death penalty if they can imagine imposing it in even one case—say, a mass murderer like Adolf Hitler. Second, some prominent legal ethicists have advised that it would be morally acceptable to lie in those cases, because the lie has the potential to save a life. These ethicists say that lying in this context fits in the moral theory of "just lies."

4. Could "reverse jury nullification" be used to convict innocent people?

No. Jury nullification only works in favor of acquittals. Once a jury acquits someone, that person cannot be tried again in the same criminal court. The Eighth Amendment makes a retrial unconstitutional. The same is not true of verdicts of conviction. If someone is convicted, and there is insufficient evidence for the conviction, he or she is entitled to appeal the case. The Constitution provides special protection to people convicted of crimes than to those acquitted, based on the idea that it is better for the guilty to go free than for the innocent to be punished.

5. How can potential jurors be informed about appropriate cases for nullification?

Every citizen should be educated about the way that our criminal justice system works—and doesn't work—including the consequences of the failed War on Drugs. Juror education, including handing out informational materials outside courthouses, is protected by the First Amendment. Citizens could also learn about strategic nullification through the media, pop culture vehicles like hip-hop music, and in their political gatherings, community organizations, and places of worship.

6. Could MLK jurors be prosecuted themselves?

It is very unlikely. Of the millions of people who have served on juries in the United States, only a handful have ever been investigated for nullification, and no conviction has ever been sustained.

Although some judges disapprove of nullification, the law makes it very difficult to remove a deliberating juror from a case, much less prosecute him or her after the fact.

7. Should MLK jurors admit that they nullified?

It's a personal decision. It sends a stronger message when people openly admit their disapproval of the law. So jurors might, after their service, post their action on a Web site operated by a criminal justice reform organization, or attend press conferences that strategic nullification organizers might hold periodically. Some citizens might not want to put themselves out there in so public a fashion, or to become formally associated with the strategic nullification movement. In that case, the inside-the-courtroom nullification and outside-the-courtroom social justice intervention would be sufficient. Courts, politicians, and prosecutors closely monitor criminal conviction rates in their districts. If enough people practice strategic nullification in nonviolent drug cases, the powers-that-be will get the message.

8. Does jury nullification lead to anarchy?

No. Jury nullification is a safety valve that the framers of the Constitution intentionally put in the document. It is part of the law. The famous historical examples—the fugitive slave cases or prosecutions for consensual gay sex or draft dodging—have not caused a breakdown in other kinds of prosecutions. They have attracted attention to their causes (and sometimes outrage), but they have not inspired widespread backlash.

9. What message does nullification send to criminal defendants?

Strategic nullification provides no comfort to violent criminals or people who victimize others. In fact, since MLK jurors would limit their nullification to a specific category of cases, it may discourage misguided nullification in other kinds of cases, like violent or property crimes. For nonviolent drug offenders, the message is safety first. The harm-reduction vision of the MLK jurors is designed to make communities less vulnerable to the injury that drugs can cause, and to keep the users and sellers safer themselves. If the punishment regime actually worked to make neighborhoods more secure, then nullification would not be effective. But as soon as one drug user or seller is locked up, another one takes their place. It would do more good to families and communities for harm reduction to replace the "lock 'em up" approach. Since every MLK juror also would be responsible for an outside-the-courtroom intervention, the message to nonviolent drug offenders is that concerned citizens are more interested in healing the community than in counterproductive punishment.

10. How long would a campaign of strategic nullification last?

The objective of strategic nullification is the end of mass incarceration and, especially, the failed "War on Drugs." When these goals have been achieved and the criminal justice system is on the right side of the tipping point—the safe side—then strategic nullification will no longer be necessary. Just as emancipation ended nullification in the fugitive slave cases, effective criminal justice will render MLK jurors obsolete. Every American should eagerly look forward to that day.

To learn more about strategic nullification and criminal justice reform in your community, go to www.JurorsforJustice.com.

5

Patriot Acts: Don't Be a Snitch, Do Be a Witness, and Don't Always Help the Police

A GRANDMOTHER IN THE BLUFFS

Kathryn Johnston had spent all of her eighty-eight years in the city of Atlanta.[1] The grandmother lived alone in the Bluffs, not quite the worst neighborhood in the city but close enough, and she was scared to death. Her neighbors tried to help her as best they could. They even went grocery shopping for her, but Mrs. Johnston was so afraid of crime that she would make them leave the bags at her door. She did not allow anyone in her house unless she knew them well.

She kept a gun to protect herself against intruders.

The intruders, three of them, came late one Tuesday night. Mrs. Johnston's green-trimmed house had burglary bars, but the unwelcome visitors pried them right off. Then the men, dressed in street clothes, began tearing down the front door.

The old woman took her pistol and fired one shot through the door. She missed. The three invaders rammed the door open and returned fire. Thirty-nine times. After they killed Mrs. Johnston, they put her in handcuffs.

The intruders were Jason Smith, Gregg Junnier, and Arthur Tesler, all officers of the Atlanta Police Department. Earlier that day they had arrested one of the many drug sellers in Mrs. Johnston's neighborhood. In exchange for leniency, the dealer wanted to make a deal. He told the police that he knew where they could buy a kilo of cocaine, and pointed to Mrs. Johnston's little house.

The officers got a "no-knock" search warrant, and that's how they ended up at 933 Neal Street on November 21, 2006. To obtain the warrant, they lied. They told the magistrate that an informant named Sam had purchased drugs in the house earlier that day. Sam, unlike the drug dealer who provided the false information, didn't actually exist. The officers knew, however, that when they claimed that an informant had provided a tip, the magistrates seldom checked the story.

With Mrs. Johnston dead and cuffed, the officers set about searching the home for the cocaine. They did not find any. Officer Smith happened to have three bags of marijuana from an earlier search, and he planted those bags in Mrs. Johnston's basement. He then called one of his many confidential informants, or "snitches," and instructed him to lie and say that he had purchased drugs from Mrs. Johnston's home.

From the start, nobody who knew Mrs. Johnston believed the police officers' story. When all the lies came to light—the drug dealer's lie, the police officers' lies, the confidential informant's lie—all three officers were charged with federal and state crimes.

Officers Smith and Junnier pled guilty to involuntary manslaughter and conspiracy to violate Mrs. Johnston's civil rights. Then, as convicted criminals, they became snitches themselves. In exchange for shorter sentences, they are cooperating with the prosecution of Officer Tesler and the investigation of the widespread misconduct of the Atlanta Police Department.

In a press conference announcing the guilty pleas, U.S. attorney David Nahmias said, "The officers charged today were not corrupt in the sense that we have seen before. They are not accused of seeking payoffs or trying to rob drug dealers or trying to protect gang members. Their goal was to arrest drug dealers and seize illegal drugs, and that's what we want our police officers to do for our community."[2]

Nahmias also said that police lying and fabrication of evidence are routine in Atlanta, and that the police department suffers from a "culture of misconduct."

This chapter is about the benefits and limits of citizen cooperation with police and prosecutors. I focus on the "Stop Snitching" movement because it is so little understood, and so crucial to public safety and the fair administration of justice. Why should you, the law-abiding citizen, want to reduce the reliance of law enforcement on snitches? Perhaps the most important reason is to prevent anyone else from ending up like Grandma Johnston.

Snitching, as we shall explore, is different from witnessing. The latter is a civic virtue. If a person has information about a crime that, in her view, poses a danger to herself or others, she should dial 911. Public safety must be the paramount concern; it is, recall, the main impetus of our challenge to mass incarceration.

But reclaiming justice sometimes requires speaking truth to power, including to the men and women in blue. The police are usually our friends—but not always. Sometimes they make requests of law-abiding citizens that are unreasonable. I will make the case that on those occasions, citizens should "just say no." Sometimes the most patriotic act is to not help the police.

THE DEFINITION OF A SNITCH

Snitches are informants who receive a reward, usually cash or leniency from prosecution, in exchange for providing law enforcement with information about criminals. Snitches are most often criminals themselves, which is how they are in a position to claim knowledge of other criminals. Snitches are distinguishable from witnesses, who, as an American Civil Liberties Union report states, "out of a sense of civic duty and concern for their communities report crime, testify as witnesses and even cooperate with police to help apprehend suspects with no expectation of payment or personal benefit."[3] The ACLU report, which is highly critical of the reliance of the police on snitches, succinctly states the difference: "Chance circumstances create a witness; the state creates an informant."[4]

One of the most notorious snitches in pop culture is the NBA star Kobe Bryant. Bryant had been arrested for rape (the case was eventually dismissed) and was being interrogated by the police. In an apparent effort to curry favor with the police and get his own charges dropped, Bryant told the police that his (then) teammate Shaquille O'Neal had been in similar situations with women, and had paid over one million dollars to prevent charges from being brought.[5]

THE PREVALENCE OF SNITCHING

We know that there are a huge number of snitches, but we don't know exactly how many. Nontransparency is one of the big problems with law enforcement's use of snitches: many police agencies either don't keep records or don't share them with the public. The evidence suggests that the police rely on snitches extensively, especially in drug cases. The FBI's budget statement acknowledges 15,000 confidential informants.[6] The DEA has 4,000 paid informants.[7]

In federal cases, about 20 percent of convicted criminals get their sentences reduced because they cooperate with the government in making cases against other people. In drug cases, the percentage rises to 30 percent.[8] In the most serious of these—i.e., those in which criminals get the most time—law enforcement's success in turning people convicted of crimes into snitches is higher still. According to statistics from the U.S. Sentencing Commission, snitches provided information in 40 percent of the drug cases in which people have been sentenced to ten years or more in prison.[9]

In state courts, where the majority of criminal prosecutions are brought, there is usually no record kept when a defendant agrees to become an informant as part of a guilty plea. Yet guilty pleas are the way that over 90 percent of prosecutions are resolved. We simply don't know how many of those deals require the convicted criminal to snitch.

Law enforcement relies so heavily on snitches for two reasons. First, informants, usually criminals themselves, are well-positioned to have reliable information about criminal conduct. Jim Bona, an assistant United States attorney in Miami, says, "If you want to infiltrate a Boy Scout troop, you'd use a Boy Scout. If you want to infiltrate a drug ring, unfortunately, you go to informants."[10]

Second, prosecutors enjoy an almost godlike bargaining power, thanks to the brutal sentences that are a feature of American criminal justice. Rod Rosenstein, the U.S. attorney for Maryland, puts it like this: "We don't appeal to their sense of civility and morality. We get a hammer over their heads. They realize that cooperating is the only way they can get out from under these hefty federal sentences."[11]

Some prosecutors describe snitching as a win-win proposition. It benefits both law enforcement and the informant. Jim Bona, the Miami prosecutor, claims that he and his snitches share "an interest to try to come together and speak to each other." The defendant wants to avoid hard time. Bona notes:

> Because of the nature of the sentences that people are facing, I think we owe them every opportunity to try to reduce their sentences. And the primary avenue of sentence reduction is through cooperation. For every story you hear about someone getting ten years, there are other people who were able to cooperate, testify against other individuals and they qualify for a significant reduction from the sentencing judge. So I know that there are people who serve the mandatory minimum and there are many other people who do not.[12]

In addition to getting a break from law enforcement, some informants get money in exchange for the information they provide — in some cases quite a lot of money. Anthony Tait, a member of the Hell's Angels, made almost one million dollars for three years' worth of snitching for the FBI.[13]

The Asset Forfeiture Program of the Department of Justice allows informants to receive a percentage of the value of crime proceeds. Tens of millions of dollars are reserved for such awards every year.[14] A San Francisco drug dealer named Edward Vaughn worked on commission for the FBI. He set up "reverse stings" in which potential drug purchasers were asked to pay in cash. When the buyers showed up, the FBI was waiting for them, and Vaughn got to keep 25 percent of the recovered money.[15]

Other paid informants don't reap quite such a windfall. Missouri police paid a drug addict and check kiter named Steve Mudd $4.65 an hour to investigate alleged marijuana offenses. His information lead to the arrests of thirty-five people. The problem was that Mudd, who badly needed money, made up the evidence. Eventually all the cases were dismissed.[16]

THE PROBLEM WITH SNITCHES

The "Grandma Johnston" case is a tragic example of a common problem. The police depend too much on the word of self-interested criminals. This reliance has several bad consequences. Innocent people are implicated, sometimes with catastrophic consequences, as in Mrs. Johnston's case. The furtiveness inherent in dealing with informants promotes corruption. Since the identity of snitches is usually confidential, there is often no way of independently verifying their credibility, or even that they actually exist. The officers in the Johnston case used this cloak of secrecy to fabricate evidence against an innocent woman.

Most significantly, the co-dependence between the police and the bad guys makes communities less safe. It tears the social fabric by turning neighbors against each other. It encourages police to make the easiest, least consequential arrests while they ignore or even reward crimes committed by the people who "help" them.

The citizens speaking out most forcefully about the dangers of informant evidence are rappers and other members of the hip-hop community.[17] Seen in its best light, the Stop Snitching movement is an intervention in the direction of patriotism. When young people translate the ideals that ignited the American Revolution to T-shirts and music videos, there is reason to be hopeful about the future of civil liberties. There are still some Americans who, like the founding fathers, are willing to stand up to the coercive power of the state. The hip-hop community's justice ideals, like those of the founding fathers, are selective and undertheorized. Still, a pop culture movement against aggressive and unreliable police tactics is more cause for optimism than despair.

Unfortunately, the "Stop Snitching" campaign has been reviled in the media. Its adherents are portrayed as violent thugs, deficient in their basic civic responsibilities. To be sure, like every political movement, the antisnitching campaign has extremists — those who would encourage noncooperation with law enforcement in any case, and even advocate violence to accomplish their objectives. These goons frequently grab the media spotlight. The rapper Cam'ron was interviewed on 60 Minutes in 2007,[18] discussing how he got shot but refused to help the police with their investigation because it was against his "code of ethics." Cam'ron went so far as to claim that if he lived next to a serial killer, he would "probably move," but he would not call the police.

More reasonable members of the hip-hop community have contested this radical interpretation of the campaign against snitches. In 2004 Rodney Bethea, a Baltimore barber and filmmaker, produced the ghetto-famous DVD about life in the hood Stop Fucking Snitching. Bethea's beef is not with ordinary citizens who call the police when they feel unsafe. To the contrary, his problem is "people that are engaged in illegal activities, making a profit from it, and then when it comes time for the curtains to close [they want to cooperate with the government in exchange for leniency]. That is considered a snitch. The old lady that lives on the block that calls the police because guys are selling drugs in front of her house, she's not a snitch, because she is what would be considered a civilian." [19]

If Bethea's distinction between snitches and witnesses sounds familiar, it's because it's essentially the same as that made by the ACLU, as described earlier in this chapter. No responsible citizen would discourage people from reporting dangerous crimes. The members of the hip-hop community who launched a national protest against police reliance on snitches are, by and large, responsible citizens. Indeed, if the hip-hop anti-snitching project is ultimately successful at reducing police dependence on paid informants, future generations may regard these citizens as true American patriots.

THE CAMPAIGN AGAINST SNITCHING

Rodney Bethea's *Stop Fucking Snitching* DVD mimicked the quick-witted improvisational form of rap music known as "freestyling." Bethea grabbed a camcorder and asked his friends to talk about what was on their minds. Snitching kept coming up— perhaps unsurprisingly in a city where more than half of the young black men have a criminal record. If the police were looking to make cases, many African American families in the city would be at risk of having one of its sons implicated by a snitch looking for a deal.

In the film, a few self-proclaimed drug dealers express disgust with people who get a break in their own criminal cases in exchange for providing incriminating information about somebody else. A man named "Skinny" pronounces snitching more prevalent in Baltimore than the HIV virus. He tells snitches, "I hope you catch AIDS in your mouth and your lips are the first thing to die." Skinny then riffs about how contributing to AIDS research is a worthy cause:

... but I'm running a foundation too. It's called "Stop Snitching in Our Communities," man. I need you to donate to me information about these bitch ass niggas so I can educate the city on what's going on. It's like health research, you feel me? So we can live and grow and raise our kids because these rats eat up everything.

Bethea started selling his DVD out of his barbershop. Critiques of snitching were nothing new; lots of hip-hop songs had blasted confidential informants by the time Bethea made his movie. The DVD's main claim to fame was a cameo appearance by the superstar basketball player Carmelo Anthony, who grew up in Baltimore.

Stop Fucking Snitching also had a merchandising tie-in: T-shirts, big and white and loose-fitting, with legends like "Don't Be a Snitch," "Snitches Get Stitches," and "Niggas Just Lookin' for a Deal." For a few months in 2005, these white "tees" were the height of fashion for African American teenagers in Baltimore.

The Baltimore police, in response, made a DVD of their own. It was called *Keep Talking*.[20] In it the police thank the makers of *Stop Fucking Snitching* for identifying drug dealers of whom they weren't aware before seeing the video. They boast that they now have arrested the camera operator as well as "people outside one of the nightclubs featured in the video."

Keep Talking concludes with an officer in a squad car saying, "So if you can find another cameraman, make another video. Go ahead. Keep on talking. We're listening." Then, with rap music in the background, shots from the *Stop Fucking Snitching* DVD are juxtaposed with images of Baltimore police making arrests, executing search warrants, and frisking a group of about twenty prisoners, all of whom are black. The men, handcuffed, stand with their backs to the camera.

CULTURAL CODES AGAINST INFORMING

Scorn for informants has been embedded in the fabric of American culture and, especially, some of its subcultures since long before the hip-hop movement against snitching. Snitching can take many forms, but the reasons people don't like it are remarkably consistent.

"Don't Be a Tattletale"

Why do parents instruct their children not to tell on others? What is the harm when brother reports sister? Tattling's principal harm is that it undermines trust. It creates a corrosive element in relationships between families and friends. No one likes to be watched all the time, even when one plans to obey all the rules. Life with a tattler is like living under a twenty-four-hour surveillance camera.

As with adult informants, the motives of child tattlers are frequently suspect. Often tattling is designed to deflect attention from one's own misdeed. The tattler's act is intended to create an alliance between the enforcement officer—usually the parent—and the tattler, at the expense of the person tattled upon. There is an off-putting whiff of hypocrisy.

The norm against tattling does not seem absolute. "Mommy, Baby Sis is playing with the gun" is likely to get a different reaction than "Mommy, Baby Sis is going in the cookie jar." Still, parents understand that the stress that tattling causes can be worse than the offense that the tattler reports. It may be that when a parent receives a tip from a kid snitch, she engages in a kind of cost-benefit analysis that is instructive to our project of reclaiming justice. If the information is about dangerous conduct, the parent welcomes the information. If the tip is about a relatively minor offense, the tattler is not rewarded. Likewise, using snitches, especially to prevent violent crime, is sometimes a useful law enforcement strategy. As discussed later, my claim is not that police should absolutely eschew snitches, but rather that they be more judicious in their reliance on them.

The Blue Wall of Silence

Before rappers, the best-known critics of snitching were, ironically, the police. They rarely report wrongdoing by their fellow officers. The "blue wall of silence" is well documented.[21] According to law professors Gabriel Chin and Scott Wells, it "prohibits disclosing perjury and other misconduct by a fellow officer, or even testifying truthfully if the facts would implicate the conduct of another officer."[22]

This unwritten code is vigorously enforced. The New York Police Department, according to a federal court, promoted "a culture of retaliation against those reporting [internal] criminal corruption."[23] Police who snitch are considered outcasts, and they may be the victims of violent retribution from fellow officers.

Maybe you've seen films like *American Gangster* and the classics *Serpico* and *Prince of the City*, all of which depict what happens to cops who snitch. The great television program *The Wire* frequently compared the disgust, shared by police and criminals, to inside informants.

Interestingly, the blue wall of silence may not function as an absolute prohibition against any kind of information sharing. One study (of English officers) found that police regarded theft by fellow officers as a worse offense than brutality or acts done to protect other officers. Officers were more willing to report crimes of enrichment than other kinds of crimes.[24] Here again we see a relativism regarding the ethics of snitching, with attention to the kind of crime informed upon.

Omerta

Members of the organized crime "families" known as the Mafia swear the oath of *omerta* never to go to the police about criminal conduct:

Whoever appeals to the law against his fellow man is either a fool or a coward. Whoever cannot take care of himself without police protection is both. It is as cowardly to betray an offender to justice, even though his offenses be against yourself, as it is not to avenge an injury by violence. It is dastardly and contemptible in a wounded man to betray the name of his assailant, because if he recovers, he must naturally expect to take vengeance himself.[25]

Omerta is an honor code; to betray it by becoming a "rat" or "stool pigeon" is to violate the "first and foremost" principle of Cosa Nostra.[26]

Omerta is absolute, which makes it different from the prohibitions against tattling and the blue wall of silence. Even an innocent man convicted of a crime is not permitted to report the real culprit to law enforcement. He exacts revenge when he can, but omerta requires him to act completely outside the law.

Journalist Ethics

Journalists are ethically bound not to reveal their sources, even when the source is tied to criminal conduct. This duty not to snitch is actually protected by the law of most states.[27] Under federal law, however, journalists can be prosecuted for a crime or held in contempt of court when they refuse to disclose sources. In such cases journalists who don't snitch are given props for adhering to their clan's code rather than the law.

A famous example is Judith Miller, who was thought by law enforcement to have information relating to possible crimes by officials of the George W. Bush administration. When Miller refused to testify, she was held in contempt of court. She served eighty-five days in jail. The New York Times called it a "proud but awful" moment for the paper, and said that "she was surrendering her liberty in defense of a greater liberty."[28] While she was locked up, Miller was visited by numerous luminaries you might not immediately associate with the "Don't be a snitch" movement, including United States senators, other high government officials, and famous journalists such as Tom Brokaw.

THE CULTURAL MEANING:
WHY NOBODY LIKES A SNITCH
(UNLESS THE INFORMATION IS REALLY USEFUL)

My claim is not that everyone unquestionably approves of all these codes against informing. In general, though, the norm against tattling seems widespread, as does the support for journalists' refusing to reveal their sources (forty-nine states offer journalists immunity from prosecution in such cases).

There seems to be less social approval of the blue wall of silence and the Mafia's omerta code, although neither seems to have inspired the same alarm as hip-hop's campaign against snitching. Indeed, accounts of the police and Mafia codes often emphasize that they are designed to promote honor and commitment. At the same time, we recognize that the codes insulate some despicable conduct. They can literally allow people to get away with murder.

Ironically, omerta seems more responsible than the police "wall of silence" because the former, at least, promotes accountability; antisocial conduct is answered, just not by law enforcement. The blue wall, by contrast, gives the police a free pass for their misconduct.

All of these cultural codes serve to remind us of the pros and cons of snitching. It is good when a child tattler prevents a grave injury or a police whistle-blower refuses to tolerate police misconduct. Sometimes, however, the cost of obtaining inside information exceeds the value of the information itself. Even when informing is socially useful, it betrays commitments and erodes relationships that depend on trust.

The cultural codes against snitching also teach us that people who refuse to snitch are not, as they are sometimes depicted, law-less. Rather, they are confronted with competing rules—outside versus inside, state versus community, external versus clan.

In any case, the movement against snitching began a long time before Grandmaster Flash started scratching records in the South Bronx. Hip-hop's campaign is part of a long tradition espoused by everyone from suburban soccer moms to "made" men.

WHAT'S GOOD ABOUT SNITCHES
(A SHORT SECTION)

Snitches, because they have access to places that the police don't, are useful. They can sometimes provide eyewitness accounts of se-rious crimes. To the extent that they are trustworthy and account-able, they can be a helpful addition to a crime-fighting arsenal.

WHAT'S BAD ABOUT SNITCHES
(A LONG SECTION)

Snitches must be used judiciously. The widespread and unregu-lated use of snitches impedes community safety. It makes the evi-dence in criminal cases unreliable. It permits police-sanctioned criminal activity. It causes lazy, inefficient policing. And it turns neighbor against neighbor in a way that undermines the social fabric.

Unreliable Evidence

To state the obvious, evidence is untrustworthy when it is provided by someone who has a selfish interest in helping the police make arrests. People who are facing tough sentences have a strong in-centive to implicate other people, guilty or not, because it is often the only way that they can get their own charges reduced.

Thousands of people have been sent to prison on the basis of mendacious testimony from snitches. Even more tragic are the executions. According to one study by the Center on Wrongful Convictions at Northwestern University Law School, half of the wrongful convictions in death penalty cases that the Center looked at were based on false testimony from informants.[29]

"Legal" Crime

Justice Department guidelines explicitly allow the police to let snitches commit any crime — including the most serious felonies — with no liability.[30] This usually seems to mean drug using and selling. Because crime in this context is deemed to be "legal," it is impossible to know how much of it occurs. Sometimes, however, police conduct crosses the line. Four New York City narcotics officers were arrested in 2008, accused of paying informants with drugs they stole from the sellers the snitches identified.[31]

For some snitches even a license to commit authorized crime is too restrictive. According to the Department of Justice's Office of the Inspector General, 10 percent of the FBI's confidential informants commit unauthorized crimes while working as informants.[32]

Inefficient Police Work: Quantity versus Quality

Ed Burns, a former narcotics officer in Baltimore, describes the problem:

> It's all about the number of arrests, and when you are generating numbers, every person [is worth] 1. You get the major drug dealer, he's . . . 1. You get the minor drug dealer, he's 1. If it takes you a year and a half to get the major drug dealer, you spend a year and a half catching one person that has a value of 1. If you go to the corner and spend five minutes catching somebody, you still get your 1.
>
> If you are a major drug dealer in Baltimore, you don't have to worry — you are not going to get caught because

nobody's looking for you. But if you are going up to the corner to cop a bag of dope, you will be locked up. We locked up 115,000 people last year in a city that has 615,000 people.[33]

This focus on the numbers creates perverse incentives. A high-level informant usually can implicate more people—generating more arrests—than a low-level informant. Low-level informants have less valuable information. Thus the high-level bad guy is more eligible for a break than the less culpable low-level offender. The bizarre result is that the police might tolerate the higher-level offense—drug dealing rather than drug using, for example—because the higher-level offenders can generate more arrests. While this might help the police make their numbers, it is clearly not in the interest of neighborhood safety.

Neighbor Against Neighbor

Just as tattling takes a toll on families, snitching puts stress on the ties that bind communities. In high-crime neighborhoods, where up to half of the young black men may have a criminal case, someone is always looking for a deal. Neighbors can't trust other neighbors, which furthers the breakdown of social organization.

A few months after September 11, 2001, the U.S. Department of Justice announced a program called Terrorism Information and Prevention System (TIPS). The plan was to recruit, as citizen informants, one million people whose jobs involved extensive contact with other people. Postal workers, delivery people, and cable installers, among others, were asked to report any "suspicious activity" they observed in the course of their work. The proposal was roundly criticized and eventually defeated in Congress.[34]

The concerns about TIPS resonate with the problem of snitches. Conservative Republican congressman Dick Armey, the House majority leader, stated that TIPS was "not consistent with free society."[35] Expecting citizens to serve as agents of the secret police seems un-American.

In addition to being a safer place, a neighborhood with few snitches would be a nicer place. We expect the government to promote norms of fair play and good citizenship, but routine police use of snitches does just the opposite. Absent some compelling public benefit, the government should not be in the business of pitting citizens against each other.

WHEN TO BE A WITNESS

People should cooperate with police in those cases in which their cooperation makes communities safer. This includes reporting dangerous crimes of violence and being willing to come to court to testify. One unfortunate result of law enforcement's overreliance on snitches is that it makes this commonsense proposition difficult in some neighborhoods. In some quarters, any cooperation with police is suspect. Indeed, some elements of the Stop Snitching movement seem to be on the verge of a bad turn—toward encouragement of witness intimidation and a general prohibition, even for "civilians," against reporting crime. These responses must be thwarted, particularly by placing appropriate restrictions on the use of snitch testimony to allay the legitimate concern that it sometimes leads to unjust results.

LEGAL NORMS AND REPORTING CRIME

While broad prohibitions against reporting crime are not in the best interests of any community, people concerned about mass incarceration and the expansion of police power might consider exercising discretion regarding the crimes they choose to report. There is, for example, a well-known nightclub in Harlem from which marijuana is sold. Customers enter, hand money to one of the bartenders, and she supplies them with pot. This is not the kind of crime for which I would be likely to drop a dime. There is no apparent threat to public safety—unlike street-corner drug selling, in which turf battles sometimes lead to violent encounters between dealers. In short, good citizenship does not require the reporting of every crime, but rather only those in which prosecution would result in some public safety benefit.

The law maintains a surprising ambiguity about the value of reporting other people's bad acts. There are few legal requirements that ordinary citizens report crimes. As explained in the next section, the law's approach here is rooted in a robust commitment to individual liberty.

MISPRISION OF FELONY

A federal law prohibiting "misprison of felony" makes it a crime to conceal a felony.[36] This statute is based on the common law of England, which, significantly, excepted family members. England abolished the crime of misprision of felony in 1967.

Under U.S. law, active concealment of a crime is required for someone to be in violation of the law. This exempts a lot of bad acts from prosecution. Michael Fortier, for example, should have reported what he knew about Timothy McVeigh's plan to blow up the Oklahoma City federal building.[37] One hundred sixty-eight lives would have been saved if he had. When he did not, however, he broke no laws. He would have been guilty of misprision of felony if he had *actively* prevented the police from learning of the plot. Thus the simple act of not going to the police makes him derelict in his responsibilities as a human being, but it does not, under federal law, make him a criminal.

Although some states based their own misprision statutes on the English common law, no conviction for a state misprision of felony offense has been upheld since 1878.[38] The practical effect is that in the United States, there is no affirmative legal responsibility to report a crime.

CRIMES OF OMISSION

Most jurisdictions do not require citizens to help other citizens, even when they can prevent grave harm. There are some exceptions; teachers, for example, must report suspected child abuse. Still, "good samaritan" laws regarding treatment of strangers are uncommon. So you can watch a blind person walk into a busy highway, or allow a baby to drown in shallow water, and the American criminal justice system will turn a blind eye.

U.S. law is different in this respect from many other Western nations. Scholars sometimes relate the difference to the more robust American concept of liberty. As the philosopher John Kleinig explains: "The fear is that Good Samaritan legislation will substantially diminish freedom. In a culture steeped in individualism, nothing produces more hysteria than measures which encroach on individual liberty. 'You owe me nothing; I owe you nothing. You stay out my way, and I'll stay out of yours.' That is an extreme expression, but it constitutes an important thread within the Anglo-American sociomoral fabric." [39]

POLICE AND PROSECUTOR DISCRETION

Police and prosecutors often know about illegal conduct and do nothing. You probably have been the beneficiary of this kind of mercy; the cop saw you speeding on the highway and didn't so much as flash his lights. Some jurisdictions have "mandatory arrest" laws for certain crimes, like domestic violence, that require the police to arrest when they have probable cause. These laws, and the crimes they cover, are the exceptions. For the majority of crimes, police and prosecutors have virtually unlimited discretion not to act, even when they have sufficient legal cause and proof.

Reporting criminal offenses is sometimes a duty of good citizenship but not usually of the law. Like the police and prosecutors, the average citizen has a broad range of discretion about voluntarily revealing criminal conduct of which she is aware. This again reflects the American constitutional value that law enforcement is not always the most important objective, and that crime detection must be weighed against the dangers of state coercion and encroachments on civil liberties.

THE LIMITS OF COOPERATION

High-crime neighborhoods are filled with . . . lots of crime. Even when citizens do come forward to report an incident, the crime simply seems to shift from one corner to the next rather than go away. In the case of drugs especially, there frequently is not a lot of mystery about who the buyers and sellers are. Any discussion of the ethics of cooperation must be grounded in a realistic assessment of the likely results.

The police don't solve most crimes.[40] As most people who have called the police to report property crime know, it seems as if they sometimes don't even try. The journalist Touré described his uncertainty about what do when he discovered a crack house in his neighborhood.[41] He wasn't enthusiastic about calling the police, because "as a black male New Yorker, I've long regarded the boys in blue as the opposition . . . and I come from the hip-hop generation, in which snitching . . . is treason."

Ultimately Touré decided to call the police. He reasoned that he wasn't a snitch because the term "truly refers to criminals ratting on other criminals, not taxpaying citizens reporting what they've seen criminals do." But then Touré discovered "it's not easy to drop a dime." He got referred from one officer to the next. Eventually the cops told him that there wasn't much that they could do and encouraged him to e-mail the police commissioner. The crack house is still in business.

THE VIRTUES OF NONCOOPERATION

Sometimes it is beneficial, in a democracy, not to cooperate with the police. One of the values of the antisnitching movement is that it reminds us that not all law enforcement is in the best interest of communities. Many African Americans are suspicious of snitches because snitches have been used to thwart civil rights movements—everything from the Denmark Vesey slave rebellion to Martin Luther King Jr.'s civil rights organizations. When the law is selectively applied, or doesn't serve to make communities safer, providing information about lawbreakers is not a virtue.

There is also a more transcendent reason not to cooperate with the police all the time. The Stop Snitching movement raises an important question that the politics of crime make a lot of people afraid to ask: How should we feel about the police? (I mean "police" in the institutional sense—i.e., the most visible civilian agents of the power of the state.) Some suspicion of—one might even say distaste for—government power is required for a democracy to flourish. How should lovers of freedom respond when the police ask us to be instruments of their authority?

When my criminal law students study the Fourth Amendment, they learn that unless the police have probable cause, they are not allowed to search.[42] The police sometimes ask citizens, especially in high-crime communities, to waive this right and permit a search of their clothing, packages, or cars. You have the right to say no (although the police aren't required to advise you of this). My cop friends boast about how good they are at getting people to consent (even, they claim, when those who consent are hiding contraband). Sometimes, in making the request, the police appeal to the duties of citizenship: "Help us do our jobs. We're just trying to keep you safe." Most people seem to go along.

I encourage citizens to just say no. I would. I should add that I do not carry illegal contraband. If I did, I hope I would have the good sense to decline consent for that reason alone. As I noted earlier, the police report that many people consent even when they possess illegal materials.

Even though a search would not implicate me in a crime, I would still say no. I hope you, dear reader, would as well. I would say no as an exercise in courage, and to send a message to the police. The message is "Leave me alone. I stand on the Constitution of the United States of America. Your gun and your baton don't scare me. I respect your work, but looking in my coat pockets or under my car seat will not make us safer."

The law says that when a person denies the police consent for a search, the police have to go away (unless they have a search warrant). My cop friends say they may not like it, but they actually do go away. But, again, most people do what the police ask them to do. Standing up to the state—especially when the state is a person with a high-caliber pistol asking you to do something—requires strength. The muscle to do it might atrophy if it is not exercised. We need the police to get used to people knowing their rights and proudly asserting them. Sometimes we should refuse to cooperate because we can. It's an exercise of faith in democracy.

6

Should Good People Be Prosecutors?

When I stopped being a prosecutor I told my friends it was because I didn't go to law school to put poor people in prison. My friends weren't surprised that I quit; they had been shocked that I became a prosecutor in the first place. For a progressive like me—a person who believed in redemption and second chances and robust civil liberties—the work presented obvious pitfalls.

"Locking people up" was practically on the job description. Eric Holder, the first African American U.S. attorney in DC, and now President Obama's choice for attorney general, asked prospective prosecutors during interviews, "How would you feel about sending so many black men to jail?" Anyone who had a big problem with that presumably was not hired.

I began the work, however, as a liberal critic of American criminal justice—the avenging Undercover Brother who would change the system from the inside. What happened instead was that I collaborated with the system's injustice.

Thinking about the business of prosecuting crimes brings questions about the utility and morality of American criminal justice into sharp relief. If there are too many people in prison, how should we feel about the men and women who put them there?

My conclusion is that prosecutors are more part of the problem than the solution. The adversarial nature of the justice system, the culture of the prosecutor's office, and the politics of crime pose insurmountable obstacles for prosecutors who are concerned with economic and racial justice. The day-to-day work of the prosecutor is geared toward punishing people whose lives are already messed up. This does not mean that criminals should be allowed to victimize others; some of the people in prison really belong there, for the protection of society. It suggests, however, that piling on is the main work of prosecutors. It is well intentioned, perhaps even necessary, but piling on nonetheless. Adding up the costs of a lifetime of deprivation and then presenting the bill to the person who suffered it seems an odd job for a humanitarian.

Also, prosecutors spend much of their time making arguments in favor of police power. They ask judges to adopt pinched interpretations of the Constitution and individual rights. When progressives bemoan the Supreme Court's approval of racial profiling, pretextual stops, widespread drug testing, camera surveillance, and police lying to suspects, they have prosecutors to thank. One of your primary functions as a prosecutor is to make the judge and jury believe the police. When the cops say that Kwame consented to the search of his backpack, and Kwame says he didn't consent, your job is to prove that Kwame is lying.

It is true that some prosecutors attempt to mitigate the harshness of the system, either openly or through the covert or subversive measures that I will discuss later in this chapter. Their principal work, however, is applying the criminal law, not ameliorating its negative effects. Becoming a prosecutor to help resolve unfairness in the criminal justice system is like enlisting in the army because you are opposed to the current war. It's like working as an oil refiner because you want to help the environment. Yes, you get to choose the toxic chemicals. True, the boss might allow you to leave one or two pristine bays untouched. Maybe, if you do really good work as a low-level polluter, they might make you the head polluter. But rather than calling yourself an "environmentalist," you should think of yourself as a polluter with a conscience.

I hope that the analysis in this chapter will be useful for any advocate for social change who ponders where she can do the most good. What is the role that our moral and political beliefs should play when we choose our work? When does compromise cross the line and become complicity? When does one do more harm than good by working within an unjust system?

A QUESTION OF CHARACTER?

Abbe Smith has zealously represented poor people accused of crimes for over two decades. She firmly believes that you cannot be both a good person and a good prosecutor.[1] She writes:

> We live in an extraordinarily harsh and punitive time, a time we will look back on in shame. The rate of incarceration in this country, the growing length of prison terms, the conditions of confinement, and the frequency with which we put people to death have created a moral crisis. Although, arguably, all those who work in the criminal justice system have something to do with its perpetuation and legitimacy, prosecutors are the chief legal enforcers of the current regime.[2]

I would not go so far as to call prosecutors "bad people." I know prosecutors who are fair-minded, concerned about economic and racial justice, and even believe that there are too many people in prison. Unfortunately, their bodies and souls are working at cross-purposes. Especially for African American prosecutors, the job exacts a terrible toll.[3]

THE CROSS-EXAMINATION

I loved it when the defendant took the stand. The judge would ask, "Does the government have any questions?"

"Yes, Your Honor!" I would leap up from the government's table, stand my full six feet three inches, and stare hard at the bad guy. On the street everybody might be scared of this dude (like they were scared of me, late at night, if I wasn't wearing my suit), but at this moment, I—on behalf of the United States of America—was running the show.

I paced the entire well of the courtroom but avoided going anywhere near the defendant. Later, if my questions got the defendant too riled up and he tried to get smart-ass on me, I would get up in his face—or at least as close as the judge would allow. For now, though, I tried to convey to the jury through my movements as well as my words that the drug dealer on trial was a piece of garbage.

ME: Where were you the night of August 5?
CRETIN: Over to my baby mama's house.
ME: What is your wife's name?
CRETIN: Her name LaShonda, but she not my wife.
ME: I see. Then you left your baby mama's house and went to stand on the street corner, is that right?
CRETIN: I saw my boy and stopped to talk.
ME: What's your boy's name?
CRETIN: Lil' Boo. I mean that's what everybody calls him—I ain't know his real name.
ME: And when you and Mr. Boo saw the police, you threw your cocaine on the ground and ran away, didn't you?
CRETIN: Naw man.
ME: No further questions, your honor.

Gentle reader, could you hear the slight hint of sarcasm in my voice when I said "wife"? Did you see my eyes roll? Every time the cretin slurred his words and tripped over the conjugation of a verb, my diction became more precise.

Here's what they don't teach you in law school: As you, the black prosecutor, button your jacket and head back to the government table, you look at the jurors and then you glance back over at the defendant. You can't actually say these words, but this is what you mean: *Ladies and gentlemen of the jury, I am an African Amer-*

ican. You are African Americans. The defendant over there—that's a
nigger. Lock him up.

I had the best conviction record in my section.

What happened to that progressive guy who joined the office?
My aspirations of changing the system got shot down because I
liked winning too much, and I was good at it. I wanted to be well
regarded by my peers, to be successful in my career, and to serve
my community. And the way to do that, I learned on the job, was to
send as many people to jail as I could. I wasn't so much hood-
winked as seduced.

THE MORNING AFTER

I feel a little bit used. The Supreme Court has written about the
significance of African American participants in the criminal justice system.[4] It seems that we perform a symbolic function, especially in cases involving black defendants. Our presence promotes
the appearance that the system is fair. The Court has stated that allowing blacks to play a role in law enforcement enhances "public
respect for our criminal justice system and the rule of law." I call
this the "legitimization function."

It is significant that mass incarceration, and its attendant gross
racial disparities, are occurring at a time when prosecutors' offices
are more diverse than ever. The United States Attorney's Office for
the District of Columbia, where I worked, has the highest percentage of African American prosecutors of any U.S. Attorney's Office.
The DC office also locks up a larger percentage of the city's black
residents than virtually any other office. A report said that on a
given day half of all the young black men in the city had a criminal
case—they were either in prison, on probation or parole, or awaiting trial.[5] Remembering the "legitimization function," one doesn't
have to be a conspiracy theorist to think the correlation between
the number of black prosecutors and black inmates is more than a
coincidence.

In DC there were many jurors who were concerned about fairness, especially about why the defendants are overwhelmingly African American. Watching the parade into arraignment court every morning, I thought of the untitled Ntozake Shange poem that begins "The suspect is always black and in his early twenties."

You had to wonder whether the 200,000 white residents of the city ever smoked pot, got into fights, or stole from their offices. The racial composition of the superior court lockup list suggests that white people in DC do not commit crimes. Does anyone who actually knows white folks believe this? So how should jurors feel about the utter blackness of the criminal court? One reason I was hired was so that people with those kinds of concerns could see my skin. It was supposed to make them feel better. To folks who had questions about racial profiling or selective prosecution, my black body answered "Everything's cool."

Everything, clearly, is not cool. Given the woes of mass incarceration and expanding police power already catalogued in this book, the shocking contention is that people who want change *should be* prosecutors. The idea that they *should not* be prosecutors seems obvious. Yet every year I entertain a parade of students who think, much as I did upon graduation from law school, that they can do the most good as an assistant district attorney. They make three claims.

CLAIM 1: PROSECUTORS HAVE A LOT OF POWER

I agree with that description absolutely; it's just that ultimately I would limit it to one prosecutor in particular. The head of a prosecution office is the most unregulated actor in the entire legal system.[6] Basically, there are no rules. There's no law, for example, that says that simply because the prosecutor knows someone is guilty of a crime, that suspect must be charged. The lead prosecutor— the district attorney or the United States attorney—can make whatever decision he wants about whether to prosecute and no judge or politician can overturn it.

The prosecutor often has more control than the judge over the outcome of a case. Sentencing guidelines and mandatory minimum sentences have reduced the discretion that judges used to have to fit the punishment to the crime.[7] The prosecutor can circumvent required sentences simply by charging a different crime, or leaving out some of the evidence. This is perfectly legal.

Federal law, for example, requires a minimum five-year sentence if someone uses a gun while engaged in drug trafficking, even if the gun is not brandished or discharged.[8] The judge who refuses to impose this sentence would almost certainly be reversed on appeal. Let's say, however, that a prosecutor doesn't want the same defendant to receive the whole five years, perhaps because she is trying to entice the defendant to snitch in another case. She can simply charge the drug case, leaving out the evidence about the firearm. No one—not the judge, not the governor, not even the president of the United States—can require the head prosecutor to add the gun charge.[9]

Line prosecutors "share" this power in the sense that they make the initial decisions about charging, plea bargains, and sentencing. As a baby prosecutor, I sometimes felt unworthy of the delegation of this much responsibility. Here I was, a kid only a few years out of law school, and cops and defense attorneys with much more experience had to suck up to me to get what they wanted. I loved it.

"Papering" was one of my favorite parts of the job. After the police arrested someone, they would bring their reports to the basement of the courthouse where we prosecutors sat in cubicles. The police would line up to talk to us, and we would make the preliminary decisions about whether or not to bring charges. We considered factors like whether the defendant had a record, if the case had "jury appeal," whether there were victims who seemed like they would be cooperative, if the statements of the police officers seemed believable, and whether there would be problems getting all of the evidence admitted in court.

I soon realized, however, that my own power was limited. Whatever a line prosecutor decides, his or her recommendation had to be approved by a supervisor. If the case was high profile or the crime grave, the review went all the way up the chain of command. Before I could proceed with my prosecution of the United States senator, for example, my co-counsel and I, along with our supervisors, had to troop to a meeting with Attorney General Janet Reno. We presented all of our evidence to her and went forward only after she blessed the case.

My concern here is not that this kind of evaluation is inappropriate; indeed, given the serious consequences of charging anyone with a crime, experienced lawyers *should* have the final say. My point is only that career prosecutors are not the people who make the decisions that have the most impact on how criminal justice works.

Here's the bottom line: rather than having "power," line prosecutors have delegated authority that is subject to several layers of review. In the federal system, the "big boss" is the attorney general, and he or she is usually not shy about reminding the legal underlings who's in charge. John Ashcroft, the first attorney general during the George W. Bush administration, reversed many decisions that lower-level prosecutors had made. He commanded federal prosecutors to appeal cases in which judges imposed lenient sentences, and, in what became known as the "Ashcroft Memorandum," he ordered his prosecutors to agree to plea bargains only when the defendant admitted the most serious charges. Bush's next attorney general, Alberto Gonzales, required prosecutors to seek the death penalty in cases in which the prosecutors had concluded it wasn't warranted.[10]

In the state system, where 90 percent of criminal cases are brought, the head prosecutor is a politician who in most cases was elected pursuant to the dysfunctional politics of criminal justice in which people get votes by promising to put more people in cages.[11] The line prosecutor has to answer to the boss, who has to answer to those politics. This limits the effectiveness of wannabe progressive prosecutors who claim that they would be more sensitive than hard-core "law and order" types. These liberal prosecutors say they would exercise their discretion to be merciful and even to not charge when that was appropriate.

The reality is that the discretion of worker bees is tightly controlled. There are certain kinds of cases that come up all the time, and for those cases there are already rules in place. A classic case of this type is that of a first-time drug offender. Virtually every prosecuting office has a procedure for dealing with those cases, and the line attorney is expected to follow the program.

In my experience, most people who work at prosecutors' offices—and especially those who reach the rank of supervisor—do not view mass incarceration and expanding police power as serious problems. To the contrary, they mistakenly believe that "tough" criminal justice makes us safer. Most will not be amenable to decisions in individual cases that are made with an eye toward locking up fewer people or limiting police power. Ultimately, the prosecutor with a social justice agenda would have to proceed more subversively than overtly.

While my experience is that line prosecutors don't have a lot of "free" discretion, there is another important limit on their power: they are stuck with the cases that the police bring. It's not as though a progressive prosecutor can say, "I don't want to try cases that are the result of selective law enforcement in poor neighborhoods" or "I want to opt out of cases that arise from racial profiling." That would be like a lawyer saying, "I want to work for a firm that pays big bucks but I don't want to represent rich people." If you are a typical prosecutor, you will spend most of your time locking up poor people. For better or worse, that's what most prosecutors do.

CLAIM 2: PROSECUTORS HELP VICTIMS

That's the goal, anyway, and it's a laudable one. It's not, however, what most prosecutors spend most of their time doing. First of all, the average urban prosecutor spends about half her time on drug cases—a crime that, at least for users, has no victim. You know

people who do illegal drugs. If you saw your friend snorting cocaine, you might ask her not to do it around you. You could tell her
you think that it's unhealthy and that she should seek treatment if
she can't stop on her own. Here is what you would *not* do: sneak off
and call 911 to have her locked up because she committed a
crime. If that is not how you would treat your friend, you should
not be prosecuting people for using drugs.

But, the argument continues, prosecutors, by convicting *sellers*,
can help get drugs off the street. Would that it were so. I wrote part
of this book in an apartment in Washington Heights, a mainly Do-
minican neighborhood in New York City. "Da Heights" still has
open-air drug markets, which in gentrified Manhattan seems so
old-fashioned it's almost quaint. In this neighborhood it's impossible to think of drug selling as victimless. I despise the dealers
standing on the corner and staring at me, unsure whether I'm
"5-0" (i.e., a cop) or a potential customer. Truth be told, I'm afraid
of them as well. It makes the streets feel unstable, like at any moment some stuff might jump off with guns blazing and schoolkids
ducking under parked cars and some innocent bystander, like me,
getting hurt. It's a perfect place from which to write a book about
criminal justice. My concern about how well the system is working is more than theoretical. Part of what I need my government to
do is to get these guys off my corner. That's homeland security at
its most urgent.[12]

But prosecutors don't seem able to rid the streets of dealers,
even in New York, home of the "Rockefeller laws," one of the
toughest narcotics codes in the country. The "replacement effect"
is in full effect. So, to be sure, they can put away Hector and
T-Bone; the next day, though, Willie, Lil' Boi, and Julio are standing there. When those guys catch their case, it's Alejandro's and
Malik's turn.

So, to reiterate the point made in chapter 3, locking up buyers
and sellers is a failed public policy. It simply does not work. That
well-meaning prosecutor sitting right now in drug court with a
hundred files on her desk? She's on the wrong side of history. It is

doubtful that in fifty years we will be addressing this pressing social issue by putting users and sellers in prison.

Other crimes do, of course, have flesh-and-blood victims. Sometimes liberals seem to ignore this truth, and that has hurt the cause of criminal justice reform. Prosecutors make people pay when they have done horrible things to other people, and that is good work. Former prosecutor Lenese Herbert remembers the day she convicted a man of a brutal rape. Even though the victim, a black lesbian, had been left for dead on the street, she was still reluctant to call the police because she thought no one would care. Lenese Herbert cared. She diligently worked the case, interviewing witnesses, sending the forensic evidence to labs, and preparing the victim for the ordeal of going to trial. When the jury returned a guilty verdict, Lenese said it was the first time she had seen this woman hold her head up high.

Still, we need to be thoughtful about how and when locking someone in a cage for five or twenty years actually helps. A significant percentage of victims, in addition to defendants, are young men who are involved with gangs or drugs. In these cases, as former prosecutor Lenese Herbert puts it, "on any given Sunday, someone who is a victim today could have been a defendant yesterday and might be a witness tomorrow." This doesn't mean that their assailants get a free pass. It just means that sometimes the line between "innocent" victim and "guilty" perpetrator is not always distinct.

I am thrilled when violent offenders, especially murderers and rapists, are put away. It turns out, however, that these cases represent a small percentage of the work that prosecutors do. Fewer than 5 percent of all arrests are for violent crimes that cause injury. You would not know that from watching either *CSI* or the local news.

The most effective long-term strategy for helping victims is working to resolve the conditions that create the crime. When we address the conditions that breed antisocial conduct, we honor victims in the most meaningful way. It's not that prosecutors don't help some victims; they absolutely do. The way that they help, though, is hard medicine with major side effects. In the end, helping victims is, at best, an occasional benefit of being a prosecutor and must be balanced against the work's considerable costs.

CLAIM 3:
WE DON'T WANT PROSECUTORS' OFFICES
TO BE TOO HARD-CORE OR ALL WHITE

Some progressives worry about what would happen if prosecutors' offices were staffed exclusively with "lock 'em up" types. They also are concerned about the prospect of segregated staffs if lawyers of color opt out of this work for racial justice reasons.

As a practical matter I do not think that all-white prosecution offices are likely in cities that have a substantial minority population. Keeping in mind the "legitimization function" described earlier in this chapter, prosecutors themselves need to have some black and brown faces in the office. There is a strategic benefit in having African American prosecutors, especially in jurisdictions in which most defendants are also African American. Just as there are always blacks like Condoleezza Rice and Clarence Thomas, who, based on their own politics, are willing to serve administrations that many others feel do not promote black interests, there will always be people of color willing to be prosecutors, even if some in the community will brand them sellouts or tokens.

A more significant threat is that liberals will refuse to work as prosecutors, leaving the offices exclusively staffed with conservative law-and-order types. If that happened, would things be even worse than they are now? What is the difference that progressive prosecutors make?

I interviewed several progressive prosecutors and most thought that their presence mattered. Even if they did not change the office culture completely, they felt that people at least acted differently around them. Two prosecutors, for example, told me that

others in the office had learned not to refer to defendants using pe-
jorative names like "douche bag" when they were around.

Every progressive prosecutor indicated that he or she treated
witnesses better than other prosecutors in the office. Witnesses are
sometimes reluctant to testify in criminal cases; they don't want to
get involved because of mistrust of the police, fear of the defendant, or not wanting to be perceived as a snitch. Some prosecutors,
to induce cooperation, yell at reluctant witnesses or even threaten
to lock them up until the trial. S.W., an African American former
prosecutor, described her discomfort at seeing middle-class white
men and women in suits shouting at the mainly poor black witnesses. She believed that her gentler tactics made her witnesses
feel better about the process and ultimately helped her win more
convictions.

"Win more convictions." Therein lies the rub. Many of the
kind acts of progressive prosecutors are, necessarily, in the service
of their work. One payoff of being nice to witnesses is that it helps
you put more people in prison.

Here's a metaphor that is extreme but I hope revealing: I understand the argument that, back in the day, slave driving would have
been an acceptable job for abolitionists. The drivers had a lot of
power and discretion, and if abolitionists abandoned that kind of
work, only hard-core racists would be available, which would
make things worse for slaves. Progressive slave drivers could bran-
dish the whip more sparingly, and perhaps on occasion cast a blind
eye while an especially deserving slave escaped.

It's a harsh comparison designed to make a point. When good
people work in unjust regimes—Vichy France under the control
of the Nazis, for instance—they must engage in a difficult calculus
of the costs and benefits of their participation. It is difficult to contain injustice when one participates in it. Society by and large rejects the argument that collaborators are helpful mitigators. We
tend to shave their heads as soon as there is a regime shift.

Finally, it is worth noting that many prosecutors, of all races and political ideologies, are committed to racial justice. They just have a radically different notion of what that means. Motivated by the "law enforcement as public good" theory, their zeal to lock up African Americans and Latinos represents their own personal attempt at reparation to the black community, compensation for all the years when crimes against people of color were not answered.[13] To believe that their solution is counterproductive, and that the mass incarceration it has caused is evil, is not to say that the prosecutors themselves are bad people. They simply don't see far enough. We can disagree about the value of their service, but we will not condemn them for it.

People with broader visions of justice, however, should ask themselves whether they went to law school to put black people in jail. Or Latinos. Or poor people. Or anyone for whom being locked in a cage will not do any good—either for us or for them. That last category consists, conservatively, of approximately 500,000 souls. For people burdened with this truth, the shame of complicity should outweigh the misguided sense of "serving" their community.

WHAT HAPPENS TO PROGRESSIVE PROSECUTORS?

People who go into prosecution with a progressive agenda get derailed for three reasons: the adversarial system, law-and-order culture, and the politics of crime.

Adversarial System

The United States legal system rests on the assumption that when two opposing sides duke it out, the truth is revealed. Most prosecutors don't see advancing the defendant's interests as part of their job; that's what defense lawyers do. Likewise, when prosecutors make arguments in favor of police power, it's not because they believe that law enforcement should always get its way. It's just that it's the other side's responsibility to argue in favor of civil liberties.

The adversarial nature of the system forces lawyers to choose sides. Progressives who become prosecutors have signed up with the wrong team. Serious challenges to mass incarceration and expanding police power not only go against the prevailing ethos of the office, they undermine the premise of the adversarial system.

Famously enshrined on the front wall of the Department of Justice is the legend that "The United States wins its point whenever justice is done its citizens in the courts." I asked liberal prosecutors what those words meant in their offices. One laughed. A couple of others said it never came up.

Most, however, said that they regarded the words as an admonition. Lenese Herbert said that when she argued criminal appeals against defendants who were representing themselves, she especially remembered her commitment to a broader vision of justice. During oral arguments she would frame the defendant's argument to the court better than he was able, before going on to present her own, opposing, argument. S.W. said that she didn't care when she lost a case because her role was just to ensure that the government's point of view was represented, not necessarily that it prevailed. Still, no prosecutor made the case that this concept served as a significant limitation on the zeal with which he or she sought convictions; at best it reminded them that they had a duty to try to prevent obvious miscarriages of justice.

The government is as entitled to a representative as any other party in court. Its business, in criminal cases, is against the accused person. That's the reason cases are styled as "The United States versus the defendant" or "The People of California versus the defendant." In an adversarial system, the prosecutor who is too sympathetic toward the defendant's plight or too suspicious of the police is not doing her job.

Law-and-Order Culture

Prosecution offices are not organized along the same paramilitary lines as police departments. Still, crime-fighting government lawyers enjoy a marvelous esprit de corps. Never before or since have I worked with people who were so glad to come to the office every day. Prosecutors and defense attorneys have this in common. Each side zealously believes that it is doing the Lord's work.

I didn't start right in calling the defendants "cretins" and "douche bags." Obviously, however, criminal defendants are not highly regarded in prosecutor offices. In many cases, this is with good reason; some defendants are stupid, some have done vile things, and others have comically bad luck. In your day-to-day work as a prosecutor, defendant sob stories about growing up in foster care, getting beat up by the police, or not being able to afford rehab are obstacles to your success.

What prosecutors have in common with most other lawyers is that they are competitive and ambitious. We all like to win. For prosecutors, that means getting tough sentences and defeating defendants' claims that the police violated their constitutional rights. Getting promoted, and maintaining the professional regard of your peers, requires keeping your eye on the prize. Shortly after 5 P.M., when the courthouse closed for the day, we prosecutors would wheel our litigation bags back to the office. Colleagues who were off the trial calendar that week were waiting for us: "Did your verdict come in?"

I might answer, in the dramatic staccato of a sports announcer describing a touchdown, "Big! Fat! Guilty!" Then there would be whoops and high fives. If I could add "jury deliberated for less than thirty minutes," I felt especially studly.

Good prosecutors don't stab notches in their belts for every victory; indeed, it is somewhat a badge of dishonor not to lose some cases along the way. If you prevail every time it means you're taking only the easy cases to trial. Still, you want to win most of the time and to be able to name some bad dudes that you are personally responsible for putting away. The culture of the workplace engenders suspicion against prosecutors with too many progressive values, translating it as too much sympathy toward defendants or too much suspicion of the police. It's not that people think you are a bad person, it's just that they wonder why you became a prosecutor.

Prosecutions and Politics

Politics plays a role in whom prosecutors charge with crimes. This seems obvious in some high-profile cases, but the following cases are only slightly outside the margins.

- Duke University lacrosse players, all white, are accused of raping an African American woman whom they hired to perform a striptease. Mike Nifong, the local prosecutor, needs the votes of the African American community to win reelection. Despite underwhelming evidence that the Duke students were guilty, Nifong charges them with sexual assault, and in a press conference, makes reckless assertions about the strength of his case.[14]
- In Jena, Lousiana, a white prosecutor charges black boys who beat up their white classmate, inflicting minor injuries, with attempted murder. In the incident's aftermath, a white youth threatens a group of blacks with a gun. The blacks disarm the white boy; they are subsequently charged with theft. The white youth who brandished the gun is not charged with any crime.[15]
- Alberto Gonzales, the attorney general of the United States, fires nine U.S. attorneys reportedly in part because he thought that they had launched too many investigations against Republicans.[16]

Like other politicians, prosecutors pander to voters. In the majority of jurisdictions, this means promising to get tough on crime, which translates to locking more people up. There are few risks to being overaggressive—even when prosecutors cross the line. Since 1976, approximately 120 people who received death sentences were later found to be innocent. In all these cases, prosecutors were responsible for these wrongful convictions. The number of prosecutors who have been disciplined for these egregious miscarriages of justice? Zero.[17]

By contrast, the line prosecutor who goes *against* the "get tough" ethos too forcefully not only risks losing her job but also risks causing her boss to lose his.

PROGRESSIVE HEAD PROSECUTORS

Sometimes liberals are elected to the position of head prosecutor. They still are beholden to politics, and to their communities' often media-driven sense of what it takes to keep them safe. Robert Johnson, district attorney in the Bronx, New York, is one of the most progressive prosecutors in the country. He has taken political heat for refusing to seek the death penalty in cases in which police officers have been murdered.[18] Still, the Bronx has one of the highest rates of incarceration in the country. I asked DA Johnson if there were too many people locked up in his jurisdiction. He said no. He regretted that his office locked up so many people, but he viewed it as a community benefit.

In San Francisco, District Attorney Terence Hallinan was a progressive's dream prosecutor. A defense attorney before he was elected DA, he believed in alternatives to prison for nonviolent offenders. He opposed both the death penalty and the Patriot Act. He refused to prosecute people for the medical use of marijuana. He said he would dismiss cases if they were the result of racial profiling. In eight years as a prosecutor, he used California's tough "three strikes" law on only nineteen people, and then only for "violent people who committed violent offenses." He refused to use it for drug crimes.[19]

Hallinan ran for reelection on a platform that included developing alternatives to incarceration for nonviolent offenders and holding the police accountable for police misconduct. His chief opponent was Kamala Harris, an African American–South Asian woman who accused Hallinan of being soft on crime. In the most liberal U.S. city, Harris, the law-and-order candidate, won with over 56 percent of the vote.

SUBVERSIVE PROSECUTORS

Harvard Law School professor Duncan Kennedy has a provocative suggestion for people who have the opportunity to work in systems that they think foster injustice. He proposed that anticapitalist associates in corporate law firms engage in "the politicization of corporate law practice, which means doing things or not doing things in order to serve left purposes." Troubled that lawyers at corporate firms "grease the wheels" of an unjust economic system, Kennedy called on associates with leftist leanings "to think of it as a requirement of moral hygiene that they defy the people they work for, and do it at regular intervals. . . ."[20]

On first impression, there is a rough analogy between people working as prosecutors who want to end mass incarceration and reduce racial disparities, and people who work at corporate law firms who believe that wealth in the United States should be redistributed. A significant difference, however, is that many socially conscious prosecutors seem to view their day jobs as part and parcel of their political objectives. They believe, as I did, they can do the most good on the inside. Radical corporate lawyers, on the other hand, see their wage-earning work as being in opposition to their political leanings (hence Kennedy's prescribed cure that these lawyers should subvert their employers). Put another way, progressive corporate lawyers want to subvert the dominant paradigm; progressive prosecutors, on the other hand, want to join it. Even the most liberal prosecutor would probably be reluctant to describe herself as "radical."

Still, the progressive prosecutors I interviewed described some conduct that their employers would probably view as seditious. S.W. recalled advising defense attorneys from time to time that rather than accept a plea, their clients should go to trial, because the government's evidence was not strong. D.T. remembered working harder for a defendant than his own attorney did to find him a drug treatment program. When A.F. wanted to offer a benefit to a defendant that his office wouldn't allow, he sometimes would tell the defense attorney, "I can't put anything in writing," but would promise to be lenient when they got to court.

Many of the prosecutors recalled ways of missing deadlines, "forgetting" to subpoena witnesses, leaving key sentence-enhancing facts out of indictments or pleas—all in an attempt to subvert the dominant "tough on crime" paradigm of their workplaces. It was striking that when I interviewed these prosecutors, in some cases years after they'd left their offices, none wanted me to use their names. They were scared. Some of their progressive interventions had to remain either secret or not for attribution—an apt metaphor for the dilemma faced by liberal prosecutors.

REFORM VS. TRANSFORMATION

In this and the previous two chapters we have considered three ways that progressives interact with the criminal justice system. To decide whether working as a prosecutor, cooperating with law enforcement in drug cases, or sitting as in impartial juror in those cases makes one complicit with mass incarceration and racial disparities requires a reckoning of two items. First, does working within the system contribute to the problem? (As should be clear by now, I believe the answer to this question is "yes.") Second, is it possible to make a real difference from inside? If mere "reform" is required, working within the system might accomplish that change. If, on the other hand, a more substantial transformation is necessary, it becomes more evident that the change must come from without. Those who work inside can tinker with the punishment regime, but they probably cannot overhaul it.

Let's say that we have two goals. First, we seek to reduce incarceration substantially. Our specific goal here is to return the United States to incarcerating "only" 1,750,000 people rather than the current 2.3 million. Our second objective is a major reduction in racial disparity in incarceration. The numerical goal here is to reduce the current eight-to-one black-white disparity to three-to-one, which is closer to the average black-white disparities in other measures of economic and social well-being.[21]

What level of change do these objectives require of our criminal justice system? The final chapter of this book proposes seven ways that these goals might be achieved. Many of these steps demand considerably less reliance on punishment as a means of treating antisocial conduct (or conduct like drug use that is purportedly outside majoritarian constructs of morality).

At a minimum, achieving these goals requires shifting the focus away from "the deliberate infliction of pain" model that now drives American criminal justice. People who now do criminal justice (i.e., punishment) work probably would describe the changes required to achieve our goals as substantial. People now employed in the punishment regime who want to continue to serve would have to engage in what prosecutors (usually derisively) refer to as "social work." Different skill sets would be required, and I daresay different motivations.

To be a prosecutor, a snitch in drug cases, or a juror who convicts in those cases simply because someone is "guilty" of the charge is to be an active participant in a system that defines too many activities as crimes, enforces its laws selectively, and incarcerates far too many of its citizens. If the punishment response had a substantial benefit to public safety, complicity might be warranted. It does not. The punishment regime creates a level of suffering—for prisoners, their families, and their communities— that should be intolerable in a civil society. An empathetic imagination of that pain—the degradation of our fellow human beings—helps us weigh the moral cost of complicity.

7

A Hip-Hop Theory of Justice

If I ruled the world, imagine that . . .
I'd open every cell in Attica, send 'em to Africa . . .
If I ruled the world, imagine that . . .
I'd free all my sons, I'd love 'em love 'em baby.

—Nas[1]

THE HIP-HOP NATION

I fell in love with hip-hop on a crowded dance floor at Yale. Everyone was screaming the chorus to the old-school classic, "Rapper's Delight": "Hotel, motel, Holiday Inn. If your girl starts acting up, then you take her friend!" It was not the most socially responsible moment for me or hip-hop, but both of us have evolved since then. We've each grown up to become experts on American criminal justice—from the inside out. You have been reading about my point of view. Now I want to add a soundtrack.

Imagine criminal justice in a hip-hop nation.[2] Believe it or not, the culture provides a blueprint for a system that would enhance public safety and treat all people with respect. Hip-hop has the potential to transform justice in the United States. Who would have thought that hip-hop—the most thuggish art—could improve law and order?

For some time the debate about criminal justice has been old-school. Different slogans—"three strikes," "broken windows," "zero tolerance"—accede to prominence, and then lose their luster.

Hip-hop offers a fresh approach. It first seems to embrace retribution—the old-fashioned theory of "just deserts." The "unwritten law in rap," according to Jay-Z, is that "if you shoot my dog, I'ma kill yo' cat . . . know dat / For every action there's a reaction."[3]

Next, however, comes the remix. Hip-hop takes punishment personally. Many people in the hip-hop nation have been locked up or have loved ones who have been. Punishment is an exercise of the state's power, but it also gets in the middle of intimate relationships. "Shout-outs" to inmates—expressions of love and respect to them—are commonplace. You understand criminal justice differently when the people that you love experience being "locked down all day, underground, neva seein' the sun / Vision stripped from you, neva seein' your son."[4]

Hip-hop exposes the American justice system as profoundly unfair. The music does not glorify lawbreakers but it also does not view all criminals with disgust. A hip-hop theory of justice acknowledges that when too many people are locked up, prison has unintended consequences. Punishment should be the point of criminal justice, but it should be limited by the impact it has on the entire community.

Now, in a remarkable moment in American history, pop music is weighing the costs and benefits of going to prison. As we listen to the radio, watch music videos, dance at clubs, surf the Net, or sport the latest fashion, we receive a hard-core message from the "black CNN."[5]

THE HIP-HOP FUTURE

Hip-hop already has had a significant social impact. It is one of the best-selling genres of music in the world.[6] Hip-hop transcends rap music: it includes television, movies, fashion, theater, dance, and visual art. Hip-hop is also big business: estimates of its contribution to the U.S. economy range to the billions.[7] Increasingly, hip-hop is also a political movement.

Hip-hop foreshadows the future of the United States—one in which no racial group will constitute a majority.[8] It is the most diverse form of American pop culture. The most commercially successful hip-hop artists are black, though there are popular white and Latino acts as well.[9] The consumers are mainly nonblack.[10] The producers are Asian, black, Latino, and white—and combinations of all of those. The Neptunes, among hip-hop's most acclaimed producers, consist of Chad Hugo, a Filipino American, and Pharrell Williams, an African-Korean American.

At the same time an art form created by African American and Latino men dominates popular culture, African American and Latino men dominate American prisons.[11] Unsurprisingly, then, justice—especially criminal justice—has been a preoccupation of the hip-hop nation. The analysis of crime and punishment comes from the people who best know those features of life in the USA.

Bold, rebellious, often profane, the music has multicultural detractors as well as fans. One need not like hip-hop, however, to appreciate its potential to transform. In the history of the United States, it is hard to recall another major form of pop culture that contains such a strong critique of the state.

Many seem to be listening. The hip-hop generation is gaining political power, and seems more inclined to use it than has historically been the case with either youth or artists. I do not suggest, however, that hip-hop fans will be a potent voting bloc in the near future.[12] My claim is more ideological. Hip-hop culture makes a strong case for a transformation of American criminal justice: it describes, with eloquence, the problems with the current system, and articulates, with passion, a better way.

POP CULTURE AND CRIMINAL LAW

Culture shapes the law, and law is a product of culture. Television, for example, has profoundly informed our perceptions of criminal justice in the United States. Most Americans can recite the Miranda warnings, not because they have been arrested, but because several times a day they observe TV cops advising bad guys of their constitutional rights.

The point that culture influences law is not new or particularly surprising. The potential of hip-hop, however, to influence law seems less obvious—perhaps because hip-hop is a product of youth culture, and perhaps because it seems to celebrate outlaw conduct.[13] I hope to demonstrate that the culture, while rebellious, can be used to inform a principled theory of criminal justice.

HIP-HOP 101

Hip-hop was born in one of the poorest and most crime-ridden communities in the United States: the South Bronx, New York. In the 1970s the South Bronx was a place of a desperate, hard-knock creativity, as evidenced by the way its citizens talked, dressed, and danced. Even the teenagers who drew graffiti on subway cars thought of themselves as artists, though the police had a different point of view.

A man who spun records for parties—DJ Kool Herc, he called himself—tried using two turntables to play copies of the same record.[14] Herc used the turntables like a musical instrument and made his own songs from other people's recordings. Sometimes Herc would speak rhythmically to his beats (a technique borrowed from his Jamaican heritage).[15] He taped these "raps" for boom boxes, and the music became popular all over New York City.[16]

Herc's work inspired other DJs, including Afrika Bambaataa.[17] Bambaataa expanded Herc's musical tracks from disco and house music to virtually any recorded sound, including rock music and television shows.[18] DJs "battled" (engaged in artistic competition) at city parks, and dancers performed in an athletic, bone-popping style called "break dancing."[19]

For the criminal-justice minded, three features of the birth of hip-hop are striking. First, many artists took what scholars call an "instrumentalist" view of the law: they didn't let it get in the way of achieving their goals. So the trespass law did not deter the graffiti artists, the copyright law did not stop the DJs from sampling any music they wanted, and the property law did not prevent DJs from "borrowing" electricity from street lamps at public parks. Second, virtually every hip-hop artist renamed himself or herself; "slave" or "government" names were seldom used to describe the artists. Many hip-hop artists named themselves in ways that seem to comment on the criminal law. A short list includes rappers and groups such as Big Punisher, Bone Thugs-N-Harmony, Canibus, Missy "Misdemeanor" Elliott, Mobb Deep, Naughty by Nature, OutKast, and Public Enemy. Third, rappers were compared, almost from the beginning, to African griots, who also "dropped science"—i.e., communicated wisdom—with drumbeats and words.[20]

In the late 1980s, rap music took two radically different directions, both with consequences for criminal justice. In one, many artists addressed political issues, resulting in, according to the *Journal of Black Studies*, "the most overt social agenda in popular music since the urban folk movement of the 1960s."[21] A classic album of this era is Public Enemy's *It Takes a Nation of Millions to Hold Us Back*.[22]

The other direction of rap, however, drew more attention, and sales. "Gangsta rap," which unapologetically depicted outlaw conduct in the inner city, became popular.[23] The group NWA (Niggaz With Attitude) received widespread media attention for its controversial song "Fuck da Police."[24]

Hip-hop music continues to exemplify a dichotomy between the political and the pleasurable. The *Washington Post* has described "two faces of hip-hop," one a "conscious" side "where political, social and cultural issues are hashed out in verse."[25] The other side is "the bling-bling, the music that embraces the glamorous life, the live-now-I-got-mine attitude found in countless hits, and in flashy videos where hootchy mamas bounce their backsides and Busta Rhymes exhorts, 'Pass the Courvoisier.' "[26]

Conscious hip-hop is critically acclaimed, with Lauryn Hill's *The Mis-Education of Lauryn Hill* becoming the first hip-hop album to receive a Grammy award for album of the Year in 1999.[27] Since then, OutKast has also won top honors.[28]

Gangsta and "bling bling" rap, on the other hand, have been derided as materialist, sexist, and homophobic.[29] Still, these forms of hip-hop have their defenders. They assert that the lyrics are accurate reflections of some people's experiences. Anyway, one person's "conscious" rapper might be another person's gangsta rapper. Bestselling artists 50 Cent, Lil Wayne, and Young Jeezy are described by some critics as gangsta rappers and by others as artists whose music comments, critically, on the costs of violence and materialism.[30]

HIP-HOP'S COMMERCIAL SUCCESS

Rap pioneers like DJ Kool Herc and Afrika Bambaataa probably did not foresee the extraordinary success their art form would have with suburban consumers. Market studies indicate that about 70 percent of people who buy hip-hop music are white.[31]

Hip-hop has also had a major impact on style. Rap stars like P. Diddy and Jay-Z preside over houses of fashion that produce top-selling menswear sold at Macy's and Bloomingdale's.[32] Hip-hop fashion started as a homage to the loose, baggy clothes that inmates wear.[33] It was even the style, for a while, to wear shoes with no shoelaces—also in tribute to prisoners, whose laces are taken away so they won't use them to hang themselves.

HIP-HOP AS A POLITICAL MOVEMENT

Some members of the hip-hop nation have explicitly embraced politics. The most prominent is Russell Simmons, the multimillionaire co-owner of Def Jam, a hip-hop record label.[34] Simmons created the Hip-Hop Summit Action Network (HSAN), a nonprofit organization "dedicated to harnessing the cultural relevance of Hip-Hop music to serve as a catalyst for education advocacy and other societal concerns fundamental to the well-being of at-risk youth throughout the United States."[35]

HSAN has emphasized reform of the criminal justice system, including the "total elimination of police brutality and the unjust incarceration of people of color and all others."[36] HSAN's focus has been the repeal of New York's Rockefeller drug laws. These laws, enacted in 1973 during Governor Nelson Rockefeller's administration, require long prison sentences for drug crimes.[37] The organization's "Countdown to Fairness" campaign is specifically intended to accomplish repeal of the Rockefeller laws.[38] The campaign is endorsed by the Congressional Black Caucus, the National Urban League, the NAACP, and both Hillary Clinton and Chuck Schumer, New York's United States senators.[39] At the Republican National Convention in August 2004, HSAN sponsored a protest rally featuring P. Diddy, Jay-Z, and Mariah Carey that attracted 20,000 people.[40]

Other efforts to organize the hip-hop community politically include the "Rap the Vote" project and the National Hip-Hop Political Convention, whose 2008 national convention was attended by over a thousand people.[41] The Internet contains numerous sites dedicated to inspiring activism in the hip-hop nation.[42]

A HIP-HOP PRESIDENT?

President Barack Obama has described himself as a fan of hip-hop. During his presidential campaign, Obama met with hip-hop artists Jay-Z and Kanye West, among others, and received the endorsement of many prominent artists. In a Black Entertainment Television interview, he said that "of course" his administration would explore how hip-hop could be used to address issues like incarceration. While criticizing the sexism and materialism in some of the music, Obama described hip-hop as "smart" and "insightful" and said that rappers had the potential to "deliver a message of extraordinary power."[43]

THE LIMITS OF HIP-HOP

I want to be careful not to overstate hip-hop's role as a political force in the United States. Compared to its cultural and economic power, hip-hop's political influence is not strong. In fact, hip-hop's primary constituent groups—young people and artists—are well known for their lack of participation in traditional electoral politics.[44] Hip-hop's role in law and policy, at least for now, will be determined more by the strength of its vision than by its community's potency at the ballot box. Its vision, though undertheorized, has the potential to transform the United States into a safer, more just society.

COMMUNITY VALUES AND SOCIAL NORMS

What happens when many of the leaders of popular culture are arrested and incarcerated? For the hip-hop nation, this is not a theoretical question. It's happened to many of its most prominent artists.[45] Both the New York and Miami Police Departments have acknowledged targeting hip-hop artists.

A revealing example of the role of punishment in hip-hop was seen in an issue of *Source* magazine, which calls itself the "bible" of hip-hop. The March 2004 cover featured the tagline "Hip-Hop Behind Bars: Are Rappers the New Target of America's Criminal Justice System?"[46] The cover showed mug shots of ten hip-hop stars who are incarcerated or awaiting trial.[47]

The statistics about rap artists reflect the statistics about African American and Latino men. In the mid-1990s, one study found that one in three young black men were under criminal justice supervision.[48] An African American man born in 1991 has a 29 percent chance of being imprisoned, compared with a 16 percent chance for a Latino man, and a 4 percent chance for a white man.[49] There are more young black men in prison than in college.[50]

The reaction of artists in the hip-hop community to mass incarceration has been to interrogate the social meaning of punishment. Prison, as depicted in rap music, is a placement center for the undereducated, the unemployed, and, especially, aspiring capitalists who, if not locked up, would successfully challenge elites. Big L, for example, complains that the police "wanna lock me up even though I'm legit / they can't stand to see a young brother pockets get thick."[51]

In order to maintain their self-esteem, the African American men who dominate hip-hop send the message that any organization composed primarily of people like them must be kind of cool; it matters not whether that organization is Howard University, the National Basketball Association, or the state penitentiary. So when people say that hip-hop glorifies criminals, it is more accurate to think of it as respecting African American and Latino men. It rejects the stigma that the criminal justice system puts on them. Since these men wield significant influence over what the nation's youth think is cool, it may be only a matter of time before punishment loses its stigma with other Americans as well.

Martha Stewart is not a member of the hip-hop generation, but when she did her prison bid, there was a hip-hop effect. She was hardly stigmatized by her incarceration; she walked out of prison and right back to her TV show, magazine, and huge corporation. It's the hip-hop view: prison is a bad thing that happens to some people, but it doesn't mean anything about their morality or worth as a person.

To say that hip-hop destigmatizes incarceration understates the point: prison, according to the artists, actually stigmatizes the government. When a large percentage of the people you know, respect, and love get locked up, then being locked up seems to say more about the state than about the inmate. We are supposed to be disgusted with people the law labels as criminals, but that would mean we are disgusted with one in three black men. The hip-hop community consists of these young men and other people who know and love them. It does not find them to be disgusting people. Just the opposite.

In a culture that celebrates rebelliousness, prison is the place for unruly "niggas" who otherwise would upset the rich and powerful. In this sense, inmates are heroic figures.[52] In "A Ballad for the Fallen Soldier," Jay-Z sends a "shout-out to my niggaz that's locked in jail / P.O.W.'s that's still in the war for real . . . But if he's locked in the penitentiary, send him some energy / They all winners to me."[53]

While idealizing outlaws is certainly not limited to hip-hop,[54] the culture's depiction of the criminal as a socially useful actor is different from, say, movies about the Old West. Hip-hop politicizes crime. Breaking the law is seen as a form of rebelling against the oppressive government. Rappers who brag about doing time are like old soldiers who boast of war wounds. The hip-hop slang for being arrested demonstrates the culture's view of the almost arbitrary nature of criminal justice: one "catches a case."[55] The language connotes the same combination of responsibility and happenstance as when one "catches" the common cold.

Some of the most exciting new thinking in criminology focuses on the role of "social norms" in preventing crime. The idea is that culture (or subculture) is more important than law in influencing how people behave. We care more about how people in our "hood" label us than how the government does. Criminal law, then, is most effective when it supports social norms that contribute to public safety. It fails when it subverts those norms.[56] The best example, as discussed in chapter 2, is the fact that when incarceration is not sufficiently stigmatized, it loses its value as deterrence.

Hip-hop suggests that American punishment is not designed mainly to enhance public safety or for retribution against the immoral. Rather, its critique of punishment echoes that of the philosopher Michel Foucault, who argued that prison is designed to encourage a "useful illegality" that benefits the state by increasing its power. The scholar Robin Kelley notes that "most rappers—especially gangsta rappers—treat prisons as virtual fascist institutions."[57]

In "All Things," Pep Love, of the rap collective Hieroglyphics, laments, "The pen [penitentiary] is an inkwell, niggaz is slaves / Even if we not locked up, we on our way."[58] When prison is thought of as a rite of passage, it has lost its potential to keep us safer. If incarceration is to be meaningful, it must be reinvested with stigma. We could accomplish this by using punishment less frequently and more effectively. Hip-hop suggests a way.

CRIMINAL JUSTICE: THE REMIX

When the prisoners began to speak, they possessed an individual theory of prisons, the penal system, and justice. It is this form of discourse which ultimately matters, a discourse against power, the counter-discourse of prisoners and those we call delinquents. . . .

—Michel Foucault[59]

Every society has seen the need to punish. The hip-hop nation is no different. Three core principles inform hip-hop's own ideas about punishment. First, people who harm others should be harmed in return. Second, criminals are human beings who deserve respect and love. Third, communities can be destroyed by both crime and punishment.

How would these ideas contribute to a theory of punishment? In a sense, the hip-hop nation, and especially its black and Latino citizens, are best situated to design a criminal justice system. The philosopher John Rawls suggests that law is most just when it is made by people who don't know how they will fare under it.[60] Imagine having to create a justice system not knowing whether you are white or black, male or female, rich or poor, citizen or alien. Since minority members of the hip-hop nation are both the most likely to be arrested and incarcerated for crimes *and* the most likely to be victims of crimes,[61] they arguably come closest to Rawls's ideal lawmakers.[62] Their theory of punishment will value both public safety and fairness to lawbreakers.

I do not mean to suggest that hip-hop culture has explicitly constructed a theory of punishment. The claim is more limited but still, I hope, profound. Thousands of hip-hop songs consider crime and punishment. These voices are worth listening to; they evaluate criminal justice from the bottom up. Our current punishment regime has been designed from the top down, and that, in part, explains why many perceive it to be ineffective or unfair.

We should not look to hip-hop culture for an entirely new justification of punishment. Hip-hop culture does not create out of whole cloth, and neither do the philosophers, scholars, and politicians who have articulated the current punishment regime. The art of hip-hop is in the remix. Thus some hip-hop overtly responds to trendy theories of punishment. For example, the "broken window" theory of law enforcement, in which the police arrest for any minor crime, has had a profound impact on the ghetto and thus on hip-hop culture.[63] Other elements of hip-hop can be interpreted as unconscious shout-outs to scholars of whom the artists probably are not aware. Foucault's influential history of the prison reverberates throughout hip-hop theory, as does the new criminal law scholarship on third-party interests in criminal law and the effects of mass incarceration. Hip-hop culture, though, is post-postmodern. In fact, some of its characteristics, especially its embrace of retribution, seem startlingly old-fashioned.

Our criminal justice system would work better if the ghetto philosophers and the classic philosophers met. They address many of the same issues in punishment, including causation, harm, responsibility, excuse, and justification. We would see that Erykah Badu, Snoop Dogg, and Jeremy Bentham have a lot in common. Immanuel Kant and Jay-Z would get along well, but their differences would be instructive. Not all of the artists are brilliant theorists, although some of them are. They represent, however, a community that has borne the brunt of the world's two-hundred-year experiment with prisons. That community knows much, has laid it down on tracks, and now attention must be paid.

RETRIBUTION AND RESPECT

I ain't God but I'll pretend.

—Eve[64]

Hip-hop abides by a strong conviction that wrongdoers should suffer consequences for their acts. The culture abounds with narratives about revenge, retaliation, and avenging wrongs. The narrator in Eve's "Love Is Blind" kills the man who abuses her close friend.[65] Likewise, Nelly warns, "If you take a life, you gon' lose yours too."[66]

At the same time, the culture embraces criminals. In Angie Stone's "Brotha," for example, she sings, "To everyone of y'all behind bars / You know that Angie loves ya."[67] The Lost Boyz rap, "To all my peoples in the pen, keep ya head up."[68] This kind of warm acknowledgment of the incarcerated is commonplace in hip-hop, and virtually unheard of in other popular cultures, which largely ignore the more than two million Americans in prison.

The most important civic virtue in the hip-hop nation is respect. One of the culture's contributions to the English language is the verb "dis," which means "to disrespect."[69] To dis someone is worse than to insult them—it is to deny his or her humanity. Hip-hop vocabulary also includes the term "props"—to give props is to afford proper respect.[70] While the misogyny and homophobia in some hip-hop makes it difficult to claim that the culture universally values respect for all persons,[71] virtually all hip-hop connotes a respect for the dignity of lawbreakers.

In attempting to reconcile hip-hop's impulse to right wrongs with its respect for dignity—even the dignity of criminals—a criminal law scholar immediately thinks of retribution. This justification of punishment is premised on the idea of "just deserts."[72] When one harms another, justice requires that she be harmed in return. Retributivists believe that punishment communicates respect for the criminal by recognizing him as a moral agent and respect for the victim by avenging his harm.

The Bill of Rights codifies the retributive concern for the criminal's humanity. The Eighth Amendment prohibits the state from punishing criminals in a manner that is inconsistent with their dignity. The Supreme Court has also interpreted the Eighth Amendment as requiring that criminals not be punished disproportionately to their crime, although it has given lawmakers wide latitude in determining what proportionate punishment is.[73]

How would a profound respect for the humanity of criminals change the way we punish them? We would be more concerned about the punishment fitting the crime. Now our sentences for drug crimes seem mainly designed to put away offenders for years.

Hip-hop culture, like retributive philosophy, emphasizes the importance of moral autonomy and free agency.[74] Both suggest that people who freely choose to do wrong should be punished. Where hip-hop theorists and traditional philosophers diverge, however, is on how to determine responsibility.

In the hip-hop view, the choice of a poor person to sell drugs has a different and less blameworthy social meaning than the choice of a middle-class person to engage in, say, insider trading.[75] In "Dope Man," Jay-Z raps, "I grew where you hold your blacks up / Trap us, expect us not to pick gats [guns] up / Where you drop your cracks off by the Mack trucks / Destroy our dreams of lawyers and actors / Keep us spiralin', goin' backwards."[76]

Hip-hop culture emphasizes the role of environment in determining conduct, whereas classic retributivist theory focuses on individual choice. In essence, hip-hop culture discounts responsibility when criminal conduct has been shaped by a substandard environment. OutKast, for example, asserts "knowing each and every nigger sellin', but can you blame / The fact the only way a brother can survive the game."[77]

The hip-hop analysis does not deny that the underprivileged are moral agents; it does, however, require us to consider thoughtfully how free some people's choices really are. In the words of NWA:

[A] *nigga wit' nothin' to lose*
One of the few who's been accused and abused
Of the crime of poisonin' young minds
But you don't know shit 'til you've been in my shoes[78]

UNINTENDED CONSEQUENCES

What you gonna do when they come for you
Work ain't honest but it pays the bills
What we gonna do when they come for you
God I can't stand life withoutcha

— Erykah Badu[79]

Punishment has had a profound effect on some American communities.[80] Think how different the United States would be if *in every ethnic group* there were more young men in prison than in college. This is the reality for African Americans.

Hip-hop is concerned with the consequences of having all these people locked up. It acknowledges that even when punishment is deserved, there may be severe collateral damage. In Florida until recently, one-third of black men couldn't vote because they have felony convictions. Across the United States there are neighborhoods where so many men are incarcerated that a male presence is palpably absent.[81]

Families, especially children, suffer the most. The rapper Makaveli notes, "My homeboy's doin life, his baby mamma be stressin' / Sheddin' tears when her son, finally ask that question / Where my daddy at? Mama why we live so poor?"[82]

Should these kinds of consequences be considered when an individual offender is punished?[83] American criminal justice answers "no," loudly. Punishment should exclusively focus on the offender. The message from hip-hop, on the other hand, is that consideration of the entire community is essential.[84]

Hip-hop culture advocates retribution, but not at all costs. If the consequence of making people pay for their crimes is the decimation of a community, then retribution is less important. Punishment should be reduced when it harms people other than the criminal.

Reducing punishment based on its effect on others sounds radical—until we look at the practice in other contexts. Under federal sentencing law, prosecutors can decline to hold corporations accountable for crimes when that would be bad for shareholders or employees.[85] In Canada a similar analysis applies to the sentencing of native people—i.e., Canadian Indians and Eskimos. The judge is supposed to consider the effect on the entire ethnic group.[86]

Hip-hop culture suggests broad support for such an approach in the United States, especially as applied to minority communities. In practice, consideration of collateral effects might lead to criminal sanctions other than incarceration—for example, probation or community service. When prison is appropriate, sentences might be shorter, or family leave could be allowed. Prisoners might be allowed to work to support their families. The goal would be criminal justice targeted not just to the individual offender, but to his entire community.

WHAT TO PUNISH?

Ain't no Uzis made in Harlem.

—Immortal Technique[87]

Who's bad?

Consider the following fact: in the United States, approximately half of the people in prison are African American.[88] If punishment is being allocated properly, this statistic suggests that half of the most dangerous or immoral Americans are black, even though African Americans make up only about 12 percent of the population. The person who has confidence in the American criminal justice system probably has an unfavorable view of blacks and Latinos, and a more positive view of whites.

The hip-hop nation rejects this view. It does not see morality or dangerousness as allocated along the race and class lines that the prison population suggests. A frequent theme in hip-hop is that the law does not correctly select the most deserving candidates for punishment. Specifically, the law does not properly weigh the immorality posed and danger caused by white elites. Rather, it exaggerates the threat posed by the poor and by minorities. From this perspective, blameworthy conduct by privileged white people or the government often goes unpunished.

Thus Ice-T jokes that "America was stole from the Indians / Show and prove, what was that? A straight up nigga move."[89] Immortal Technique complains that "families bleed because of corporate greed."[90]

Hip-hop artists sometimes accuse the state of complicity in crime. In "Gun Music," Talib Kweli raps, "You know who killing it, niggas saying they militant / The only blood in the street is when the government spilling it."[91] In another song, Kweli provides an example: "[The police] be gettin' tips from snitches and rival crews / Doin' them favors so they workin' for the drug dealers too / Just business enforcers with hate in they holsters / Shoot you in the back, won't face you like a soldier."[92]

Of course, complaints that criminal law is selectively enforced against blacks and other minorities are familiar, and not only in hip-hop culture. Hip-hop's indictment of criminal justice goes further; it identifies bias in the way that crime is defined as well as the way that the law is enforced.

Some hip-hop artists have suggested that lawmakers define crime in a way that does not challenge powerful corporate interests, even when corporations cause harm. KRS-One, in "Illegal Business," explains: "In society you have illegal and legal / We need both, to make things equal / So legal is tobacco, illegal is speed / Legal is aspirin, illegal is weed."[93] It is legal for a corporation to make a gun. Nicotine and alcohol distributors are licensed by the government; in the case of tobacco there are even government subsidies for growers. Sellers of other drugs, including arguably less harmful ones, are punished. Hip-hop suggests that some of the existing distinctions between legal and illegal conduct, and between crimes and torts, are unprincipled.

Hip-hop sometimes presents poor minorities as relatively powerless in the grand scheme. "Right or wrong . . . I don't make the law," Erykah Badu explains to her criminal-minded lover in "Danger."[94] In this view, the real bad dudes—including people who profit from widespread alcoholism, tobacco sales, and the demand for guns—are politically powerful. The fact that their injurious conduct is not punished helps explain hip-hop's lack of confidence in American criminal justice.

HIP-HOP AND DRUGS: KEEPING IT REAL

In hip-hop culture, the idea that minorities are selectively prosecuted[95] sometimes seems to border on paranoia. In the case of drug offenses, however, this perception is accurate. According to statistics compiled by the U.S. government, blacks represent about 14 percent of monthly drug users. Yet they account for more than 56 percent of people incarcerated for drug use.[96] Just because you are paranoid, the old joke goes, doesn't mean they're not out to get you.

The fact that drug offenses are selectively prosecuted in the African American community informs the hip-hop perspective on drug criminalization, but it is only one factor among many. Some people say that hip-hop glorifies the use of illegal drugs. This is partly true.

Hip-hop culture suggests that recreational drugs like marijuana and Ecstasy enhance the quality of life and that they are fun.[97] Hip-hop stars Ja Rule, Missy Elliott, and Tweet collaborated on a song called "X," which extols the virtues of having sex under the influence of Ecstasy.[98] The Notorious B.I.G. raps: "Some say the x, make the sex / Spec-tacular."[99]

Marijuana, especially, is the hip-hop nation's intoxicant of choice. In a classic song, Snoop Dogg raps about the pleasure of riding through his neighborhood sipping alcohol and smoking weed.[100] The scholar Michael Eric Dyson describes marijuana as "the necessary adjunct to ghetto fabulousness. . . . Getting high is at once pleasurable and political: It heightens the joys to be found in thug life while blowing smoke rings around the constraints of the state."[101]

There are more hip-hop songs critical of the harm posed by alcohol than by other soft drugs. The most vilified drug might be the "40 ounce." Public Enemy, for example, compared this large can of malt liquor that is sold almost exclusively in poor neighborhoods to a "gun to the brain."[102]

Hip-hop offers a more nuanced, and less consistent, perspective on "hard" drugs. The sellers are accorded more respect than the users. Rapper 2Pac (aka Tupac Shakur), for example, criticizes his addict parent for being a "part-time mutha."[103] In another song, however, he praises street-corner dealers for raising him when his father was not present.[104]

Other hip-hop artists are angrier at drug sellers. Ice Cube raps, "And all y'all dope-dealers . . . You're as bad as the po-lice — cause ya kill us."[105] He goes on to castigate dealers for "exploitin' us like the Caucasians did / For 400 years — I got 400 tears — for 400 peers / Died last year from gang-related crimes."[106]

Still, there is sympathy for why some people sell drugs. Biggie Smalls facetiously dedicated his autobiographical song "Juicy" to the people who called the police when he was "just tryin' to make some money to feed my daughters."[107] Kanye West raps about being "forced to sell crack" because there "ain't no tuition for having no ambition / and ain't no loans for sittin' your ass at home."[108]

Ultimately, hip-hop acknowledges the terrible consequences that some drugs have for individuals and communities. The culture is not as quick as some scholars to label drug crimes "victimless." Acknowledging these costs, however, does not necessarily lead to a belief that drug offenders should be punished. The hip-hop consensus seems to be against punishment of drug offenders, because of (1) the selective enforcement of the drug laws in minority communities; (2) the social factors that contribute to drug use and sales; (3) the fact that the government allows the sale of harmful drugs like tobacco and alcohol; (4) the government's perceived complicity in the availability of drugs in the ghetto; and (5) the collateral consequences of punishment in minority communities.[109] In this view, the state may have a legitimate interest in controlling the use and sale of some drugs. First, however, the government must prove that it can enforce the drug laws in a nondiscriminatory way and that the benefits of regulation will not be outweighed by the costs.[110]

PRISON

> I hold this slow and daily tampering with the mysteries of the brain, to
> be immeasurably worse than any torture of the body.
>
> — Charles Dickens[111]

The idea of using prison to punish people is only about 200 years old. It was intended to be more humane than the then-prevailing methods of punishment: killing criminals, harming their bodies, or banishing them from the country.

How successful has the experiment been? The hip-hop nation is better situated to answer the question than virtually any other community in the world. The United States incarcerates more people per capita than any country in the world.[112] The majority of its inmates are African American and Hispanic. Hip-hop became popular during the same period that the prison population experienced its greatest expansion.

The experiences of the over two million people now incarcerated in the United States have been documented more in hip-hop than in any other medium. The portrait is ugly. To Nas, prison is "the belly of the beast" and "the beast love to eat black meat / And got us niggaz from the hood, hangin' off his teeth." [113]

The universal view is that punishing people by locking them in cages for years is a miserable public policy. Incarceration is cruel because it is dehumanizing. It is counterproductive because, as discussed earlier, it has been used so promiscuously in minority communities that it has lost its value as deterrence. The scholar Robin Kelley summarizes the hip-hop perspective as follows: "Prisons are not designed to discipline but to corral bodies labeled menaces to society; policing is not designed to stop or reduce crime in inner-city communities but to manage it." [114]

The artists put it more poetically. In the words of Dead Prez, "Behind enemy lines, my niggas is cellmates / Most of the youth never escape the jail fate / Super maximum camps will advance they game plan / To keep us in the hands of the man locked up." [115] Immortal Technique says that "sleeping on the floor in cages starts to fuck with your brain / The system ain't reformatory, it's only purgatory." [116] DMX describes "the frustration, rage, trapped inside a cage." [117]

Hip-hop often depicts incarceration as being driven by profit rather than public safety. Its analysis is that it is socially expedient to warehouse people whose problems are difficult or expensive to treat, especially when there are economic benefits to the (largely white and rural) communities where prisons frequently are situated.

The hip-hop perspective is reminiscent of the philosopher Immanuel Kant's concern that it is immoral to punish people as a means of benefiting society. According to some artists, that is the real meaning of the punishment regime. Gang Starr complains: "The educational system presumes you fail / The next place is the corner then after that jail." [118] Mos Def suggests a "prison-industry complex" that supports a "global jail economy." [119] Ras Kass explains: "It's almost methodical, education is false assimilation / Building prisons is more economical." [120]

WORD IS BORN

Hip-hop culture ascended to national prominence in the post–civil rights era. For the hip-hop nation, one of the enduring lessons of the civil rights movement is that the criminal law was used as an instrument of racial subordination. Images of civil rights activists getting locked up, or beat up by the police, are common in hip-hop culture, especially music videos.

Hip-hop artists express some of the same concerns as do traditional civil rights activists about criminal justice. Both vigorously protest racial profiling by police. Unlike civil rights culture, however, hip-hop is not focused on proving respectability to elites. As an NAACP civil rights lawyer, Thurgood Marshall, based on this "politics of respectability," refused to represent black men accused of raping white women, even when he thought they were innocent. Hip-hop doesn't care as much about what the rich and powerful think. It champions the human rights of those society chooses to call criminals as enthusiastically as the rights of the falsely accused. It is as concerned with fairness for drug sellers as for law-abiding middle-class people who are stopped by the police for "driving while black" or "driving while brown."

One serious deficiency in hip-hop is its endemic sexism and homophobia. Can any credible theory of justice be based on a culture that routinely denigrates more than half the population? The answer must be "no." For hip-hop to command the moral authority that, at its best, it deserves, it must address subordination within the hip-hop nation. The problem besmirches hip-hop's extraordinary aesthetic achievement and detracts from its important evaluation of criminal justice. Hip-hop music and videos, especially, contain the kind of depictions of gender and sexuality that we might expect of adolescent boys.

The increasing prominence of women rappers provides limited cause for hope.[121] Hip-hop has a long way to go, however, before its constructive political analysis is not compromised by lyrics, visual images, and attitudes that put down a considerable portion of its own community.

This chapter is a beginning. It is an attempt to fashion a hip-hop jurisprudence. In hip-hop culture there is a tradition of answer raps—of provocative responses to provocative words. I look forward to those responses.

8

Droppin' Science: High-Tech Justice

New technology is often presented as the enemy of civil liberties. It isn't, necessarily. We can use developments in science to help make us safe and free. Technology can be employed to punish people more humanely. It can reduce the number of people in correctional facilities. It can enable less police intrusion on innocent people.

I am still a prosecutor at heart. I believe that when people hurt others there should be consequences. My quarrel with American criminal justice is simply that we are going about it the wrong way—punishing too many people for too many things. Science can help us get it right.

There are at least three ways that technology can be employed to remedy mass incarceration and regulate police power. First, it can create alternatives to prison. Second, it can help prevent or reduce the behavior that lands people in prison. Third, it can help the police enforce the law in ways that are more protective of individual rights.

All of the technology described in this chapter would provide the government more information about our personal lives. That prospect seems frightening at first, and potentially oppressive. As chapter 2 points out, democracy depends on a healthy distrust of government decision makers; if they know too much about us, we feel vulnerable. I am sympathetic to these concerns; indeed, I share them. The problem is that technology, and the government's use of it, cannot be contained—even for the best reasons.

People opposed to mass incarceration and the expansion of police power have two choices. The Luddite alternative is to ignore technology, or to bemoan it, and ultimately to be its victim. The more progressive choice, I think, is to embrace the science and channel it toward humanitarian ends.

Imagine how the specter of the World Wide Web would have sounded during the 1960s. Certainly there would have been concerns about privacy. Even now, Internet users probably don't appreciate the consequences of revealing our every click to Google and Time Warner. Yet the Internet has advanced civil liberties in important respects. It is a low-cost mass medium that has connected people, and causes, all over the world. It's difficult now to imagine political organizing, including the election of President Barack Obama, without it. Resistance to the WWW would have been futile, so what advocates for social justice did was to make it work for them. We must have the same goal as we investigate the future of criminal justice technology.

AN ALTERNATIVE TO PRISON:
ELECTRONIC MONITORING

A transponder is surgically implanted inside the arm of a convicted criminal. A GPS satellite surveillance system allows the police to track him where ever he goes. If he leaves the allowed areas—his home and workplace—the transponder alerts the police.

We're not quite there yet. But the question isn't *whether* high-tech devices are going to be used in place of incarceration, it's *how*. For the last twenty years, "home confinement" has become increasingly popular.[1] Part of the reason for the growing acceptance of home confinement is that it works better than prison. The commonsense proposition is that changes in behavior can be effected better and more economically by treatment in "the offender's natural environment" rather than by institutional care.[2] The criminologist Thomas Toombs notes that prisons reinforce, rather than modify, negative behavior. High-tech electronic monitoring, on the other hand, would allow correctional workers to "help offenders learn how to act acceptably in the real world, rather than [in] the unreal world of a prison."[3]

Home detention is much less expensive than prison. According to the U.S. Bureau of Prisons, the average daily cost of federal incarceration is $64.32 per prisoner, while the average daily cost of home confinement with electronic monitoring is $17.95.

Ankle Bracelets and Other Accessories

Electronic Monitoring (EM) refers to the equipment that is used to monitor compliance with a home detention sentence. There are two categories of EM devices. The first is a continuous signaling system, which requires both a transmitter, usually in the form of a device worn around the wrist or ankle, and a receiver-dialer, which is installed on the offender's home phone line. The transmitter sends a continuous signal to the receiver-dialer, indicating that the offender is at the monitored location. If this signal is broken, or if the transmitter is removed, the receiver-dialer automatically calls the monitoring agency and informs them of a violation.

The second type of EM is a programmed contact system. Periodic calls (either by a person or a machine) are made to the offender's home to verify his presence. The offender responds to assure the monitoring agency of compliance. Methods of verifying a response include an "electronic handshake" made by inserting a device into equipment attached to the telephone, voice verification technology that analyzes the offender's voice over the phone line, and acoustic codes transmitted by devices worn on the offender's body.

Home confinement punishment can range from "curfew," in which the offender must be at home by a certain time every evening, to "home detention," in which the offender must remain at home except to go to work, school, or rehab appointments. The most severe confinement is known as "home incarceration." In this case, the prisoner must always remain at home except for court dates or medical emergencies.

Popularity of Electronic Monitoring Programs

Under federal law, home confinement is authorized as a condition of pretrial release, probation, parole, or supervised release. It is not an authorized sentence in and of itself.[4]

States, on the other hand, use EM more creatively. Programs vary in objectives and target groups. Some are limited only to particular groups of offenders, such as drunk drivers, while others focus on a particular point in the criminal justice system, such as probation. Some programs exist only for high-risk groups, while others are available only to low-risk groups, such as first-time offenders.[5]

These programs are growing rapidly. In 1987, only 826 offenders across the country were electronically monitored. By 1998, that number had grown to more than 95,000.[6]

Electronic monitoring is also a feature of justice systems outside the United States. It already is well-established in England, Sweden, and the Netherlands. Pilot programs exist in Belgium, France, Germany, Italy, Portugal, Switzerland, and Spain.[7]

Most electronic monitoring systems, in the United States and abroad, are developed and managed by private companies.

Advances in Electronic Monitoring Technology

Recent advances are making the electronic monitoring of criminals even cheaper and more effective than imprisonment. Up to now electronic monitoring has been accomplished mainly by using ankle bracelets. These devices raise an alarm if they are removed or the subject is more than fifty feet from the receiver-dialer attached to the telephone. Media mogul Martha Stewart, under home detention as part of her parole, sometimes wandered too far away from her receiver-dialer as she gardened on her Connecticut estate. There was usually much television footage of the resulting police response, sirens blaring.

The great EM quest is to unshackle the offender from the telephone.[8] This would make constant monitoring possible no matter where she goes.[9]

Such technology is already being used by biomedical researchers to track animals. The animals are implanted with microprocessor-based systems that emit signals. The devices and the implantation, done by syringe, are inexpensive and comparatively low-tech.

The development of microchips for humans is already under way. U.S. patents have been obtained for microchips implanted in teeth and for a scanner-read identification tag worn outside the human body.

One example is the VeriChip, marketed by Applied Digital Systems. The VeriChip looks like a grain of rice. In a surgical procedure, the chip is embedded in a person's skin, usually around the upper arm. Each chip contains a sixteen-digit ID number. Though the chip is invisible to the human eye, it can be scanned and linked to information about the implantee. It is the first, and so far only, microchip approved by the FDA for human implantation.

SmartDevice, a microchip manufactured by a subsidiary of Hughes Aircraft Company, awaits FDA approval. It is a "passive" transponder (meaning it does not have its own power source) that can be activated by low-frequency radio waves. SmartDevice can do more than the VeriChip; its capabilities include storing data, "adverse event reporting," and surveillance. Clinical tests have already begun in Europe.

HOW WELL DOES EM WORK?

A study, limited to less-serious offenders, found that recidivism was reduced when the punishment was a short jail stint followed by a period of electronic monitoring. Recidivism was higher for people who were punished with jail alone. The study suggested that EM works because it simultaneously affirms the offender's place and identity within the community while causing shame for having committed the crime.

An article published in the *University of St. Louis Law Journal* notes that the "principles of social learning and self-efficacy theories suggest that the likelihood of successful behavior modification may be enhanced if the offender remains and is treated, but not merely placed, in the setting to which the confinee would traditionally return" at the end of his sanction.[10] Where do most inmates go when they get out of prison? Home. If their punishment requires them to remain there, the evidence suggests that they are more likely to do the right thing.

Not all of the reports on high-tech EM have been positive. Perhaps not surprisingly, there are health concerns about implanting microchips in humans. Some studies have linked microchips to malignant tumors in animals.[11] Almost all of these studies have involved laboratory mice. Thus far, microchips don't seem to impose the same risks on either dogs (tens of thousands of household pets have implanted microchips to allow their owners to track them if they get lost) or the approximately two thousand people in whom chips have been planted. Scientists say that more research is needed before the technology is used extensively in humans.

Even if it can be done safely, EM has another downside. Professor Dorothy Kagehiro has pointed out that it may create or exacerbate a two-class criminal justice system: one for the affluent and one for the poor. Home confinement requires, at a minimum, that you have a home. Some jurisdictions also make the offender pay the equipment installation fees. It would perpetuate existing inequities if home confinement becomes a punishment for the wealthy, while poor people have to endure incarceration. Professor Kagehiro also observes that EM has less of a deterrent effect on white-collar crimes. Many such crimes take place over the phone or the Internet, all easily accomplished under a sentence that is served at home.

Should social justice advocates embrace the idea of implanting chips in people so that they can be tracked (if this procedure can be proven to be safe)? Absolutely, if the alternative is to lock them in a cage. By almost any measure, U.S. prison sentences are too long, and some crimes don't need to be punished with prison at all. Still, punishment is a cultural phenomenon as well as a legal and political one. We like it, in the United States. I, the former prosecutor, daresay that we need it. But we also should do it as humanely as possible. We obviously don't want to punish in a manner that is counterproductive to public safety. More study of the consequences for various kinds of offenders is required. High-tech EM has the potential to keep hundreds of thousands of people out of correctional facilities, and genuinely to aid in their rehabilitation.

DRUGS FOR DRUGS

The five most addictive drugs: alcohol, nicotine, cocaine, heroin, and amphetamines[12]
Number of American addicts: 22,000,000[13]

Prosecuting addicts was almost too easy. The poor ones—the people who usually get caught—look like . . . well, they look like junkies. Even if an addict didn't take the stand in his own defense, the subtext of my closing argument to the judge or jury often was "Look over there. Just look at him. Gross, right? Send him to jail."

Because the War on Drugs has been, in part, a war of propaganda, we think of addicts as weak, vaguely immoral, lazy at best—lacking sufficient willpower to conquer their nasty "habit." If they were only disciplined enough, they would be able to change their car-radio-stealing, Ensure-swilling, fare-beating, squeegee-washing ways.

Although only a small percentage of drug users become addicts, the addicts are responsible for quite a bit of crime.[14] If there were an effective way to treat addiction, we could make neighborhoods safer and reduce incarceration by preventing crime. We could end the misery—family dysfunction, lost economic productivity, auxiliary health issues—that drug dependence causes. The ideal treatment would be one that didn't require much effort or motivation on behalf of the addict. A good treatment would be a pill, or an injection. A vaccine would be even better.

Medication to treat addiction seems, at first blush, counterintuitive. It makes addiction sound like diabetes, or depression. But drug dependence is a lot like a chronic physical condition. As with many diseases, there is a genetic component; addiction tends to run in families. There's a biochemical aspect as well. Addicts' brains are built differently, in some important ways, than the brains of nonaddicts. All this suggests that addiction, like any other illness, is more effectively cured by medicine than punishment.

The National Institute on Drug Abuse and the National Institute on Alcohol Abuse and Alcoholism are testing more than 200 addiction medications.[15] They range from drugs that improve "willpower" to those that reduce the powerful effect of cues that stimulate drinking, to those that eliminate the intoxicating effects of drugs.

Drugs to treat addiction aren't new, but until recently there hasn't been a drug that has worked well. The most famous antiaddiction narcotic is methadone. It helps people get off heroin but is itself addictive. Similarly, Antabuse, a pharmaceutical treatment for alcoholism, has been around for fifty years. It makes people throw up if they drink liquor. The problem is that if you're a committed alcoholic, you simply don't take it when you want to drink. For that reason, it has not been widely prescribed.

A new alcoholism treatment, Vivitrol, seems more promising. It prevents someone from getting drunk, no matter how much he or she drinks. Best of all, it's administered in an injection whose effect lasts for weeks at a time. The advantage is that this deters impulsive drinking; an alcoholic can't turn off the effect of Vivitrol to get drunk for a night.

Studies are ongoing to find similarly acting pharmaceuticals to treat dependence on other drugs. Vaccines against cocaine, heroin, and methamphetamine addiction are being tested. They work essentially the same as Vivitrol does, by preventing users from becoming high.

Another new drug, Vigabatrin, regulates brain chemistry to treat cocaine and methamphetamine addiction. Since addicts have less of a neurotransmitter called GABA, Vigabatrin blocks the intense intoxicating effect of cocaine and meth and reduces craving by increasing GABA levels.[16] In a clinical trial, 30 percent of Vigabatrin patients avoided cocaine, compared with 5 percent in a control group.[17]

Antiaddiction drugs advance social justice in three ways. First, their success in reducing addiction offers compelling evidence that narcotics are better dealt with through public health measures than in the criminal justice system. Second, as unemployed or low-income addicts are cured, they stop committing crimes to support their habits. This makes the streets safer for everyone. Third, as they are treated, addicts stop going to prison (at least for drug crimes). It is safe to say that many of the 500,000-plus people now locked up for drug offenses would not be there if there were a cure for addiction. How ironic that the mass incarceration caused in part by the War on Drugs might be remedied by drugs.

Rarely is any disease completely cured by one magic pill, and addiction is a particularly complicated disease. Addicts would probably need therapy as well as pharmacologic treatment. Still, as a treatment for drug users who want to stop but can't, these drugs hold tremendous promise.

In terms of good public policy, electronic monitoring and antiaddiction drugs are no-brainers. They will reduce incarceration and enhance public safety. Their costs in terms of civil liberties pale in comparison to the civil liberty infringements of incarceration, and they treat people who have made mistakes with more respect and dignity than prison. The technologies in the next group, however, are more problematic. Rather than recommending them, I am proposing a conversation about whether, and how, they can be employed to reduce incarceration and enhance freedom. They also have, I'll acknowledge, the potential to make things worse. Whether we are ready or not, however, the following technologies are on their way. The hope is that by being proactive advocates for social justice, we can mediate the harm and accentuate the good.

LOOKING FOR DRUGS IN ALL THE RIGHT PLACES

In chapter 3, I pointed out that the single best way to reduce incarceration and decrease violent crime, would be to decriminalize drugs. People should not be punished for buying and selling small amounts of narcotics. It seems unlikely, though, that the police will abandon enforcement of the drug laws anytime soon. Unfortunately, one of the victims of their misguided strategy is the Bill of Rights, especially the Fourth Amendment's prohibition against unreasonable searches and seizures. Pretextual stops, racial profiling, "consent" searches—all are rooted in the police trying to find drugs. If law enforcement had a way of looking for drugs less intrusively, innocent people, especially in high-crime neighborhoods, would not suffer so many privacy deprivations.

Enter the "electronic nose." A prototype device developed by Georgia Tech scientists sends off an electronic signal if cocaine is present in a room.[18] The United States Customs Service and the Office of National Drug Control Policy supported the research.[19] The E-Nose works like a drug-sniffing dog, only more accurately. Canines can be thrown off by substances that are molecularly similar to cocaine, like caffeine.

The electronic nose "knows." According to its creators, it can detect a tiny fraction of a drug. It uses a quartz crystal to measure the unique sound wave that every chemical compound generates.

(NASA has developed another prototype "ENose" that is so sensitive it recognizes the difference between Pepsi and Coke!)[20]

The specter of the drug-detecting E-Nose raises important concerns. These techniques actually have the potential to *increase* incarceration. Now, only a small percentage of people who use drugs get caught; the E-Nose would expose many more. This would have the interesting, and beneficial, potential to equalize drug law enforcement and reduce racial disparities. African Americans, I have already noted, don't use drugs more than other racial groups. In the United States, they account for about 14 percent of illegal drug users, and yet they represent almost 56 percent of people who are incarcerated for drug offenses. One reason for this is that lawmakers punish "black" forms of drugs like crack cocaine more severely than "white" forms like powder cocaine. But the most important reason is the selective enforcement of drug laws in the African American community. E-Nose could reduce this selective enforcement.

Overall the E-Nose would offer more protections to people who don't use illegal drugs; they would be subject to fewer intrusions by the police. There would, however, be greater invasions of privacy of people who do use illegal drugs but who now evade the attention of the police — quite a lot of people.

This technology is on its way. A thoughtful reckoning of its costs and benefits would be more productive, and ultimately more protective of civil liberties, than a knee-jerk reaction against it. Moreover, since 100 percent detection schemes like speed sensors and red-light cameras are generally unpopular, the specter of universal drug detection could advance the political case for the decriminalization of drugs.

BRAIN SCANS

Police sometimes impinge on civil liberties not only when they look for evidence, but also when they conduct interrogations. A confession is, from the point of view of police and prosecutors, the best way to solve a crime. The police are very good at getting suspects to talk, even after they give suspects Miranda warnings, which basically are an admonishment against talking. (For the record, I don't know any criminal lawyer—prosecutor or defense attorney—who would consent to talk to the police immediately after they were arrested, regardless of whether they were innocent or guilty.)

Officers get people to talk by methods that include lying about the evidence in the case, lying about witnesses, and lying about the likelihood of prosecution, among other things. Bad cops go even further; they may threaten suspects with violence, or torture them, unless they confess.

Imagine a lie detector that had close to 100 percent accuracy. We're not nearly there yet, but science is getting closer. Can the Orwellian-sounding technique of "brain scanning" enhance public safety and promote civil liberties? Some scholars have suggested that fMRI (functional magnetic resonance imaging) scans, which are much more reliable than traditional lie detectors, will do away with interrogation and torture, while others argue that they will lead to a sinister future.

Current Technology

Polygraphs work by measuring body changes, like blood pressure and heart rate, that are associated with lying. They are not especially reliable at detecting dishonesty because they actually measure stress, which even honest people can experience when they have to take a lie-detector "test." A dishonest person, on the other hand, can "fool" the polygraph by not showing signs of stress.[21]

In 2002, the National Academy of Sciences concluded that polygraph results are too unpredictable to be used for security screening at national labs. Despite this, the Department of Defense, FBI, CIA, and NSA continue to administer thousands of polygraph tests each year to job candidates and those seeking security clearance.[22]

fMRI Brain Scans as Lie Detectors

For better or worse, a much more accurate lie detector is on its way. Functional magnetic resonance imaging has been used for medical treatment and research since the early 1990s. This kind of brain scan literally shows what is going on in someone's mind.[23]

You lie down in a big magnetic contraption. Electrodes are placed around your head; they measure your brain waves to see which parts of your mind are most active when you are asked particular questions. The resulting scans reveal how hard you were thinking and the part of your brain—for example, the part that deals with memory or the part that deals with planning—you used to answer the question. It's like a printout of your mind.

We're not there yet. But advocates suggest that research will yield a "nearly foolproof lie detector" in the future. Professor Richard Wiseman from the University of Hertfordshire explained that the discrepancy in brain activity results from the nature of lying. Good lying, he notes, is cognitively quite hard. "You have to think what is plausible, what does the person know, what they can go and check on, and so on. So, in terms of brain activity, the indicators are likely to be more reliable."[24]

Marketing and Development

Private companies have already been formed to commercialize the brain-scanning work being done at the universities. These companies claim that current fMRI tests can spot liars with 90 percent accuracy. They also suggest that this level of accuracy will only improve with time, eventually approaching a negligible margin of error.[25] The companies have relied, in part, on recent research funded by the federal government aimed at producing a foolproof method of detecting deception. This funding became available after the 9/11 attacks, with support from the FBI, CIA, the Department of Defense, and other agencies.

Limitations

There are lots of problems with fMRI technology in its current state, problems that would prevent its reliable use in a criminal investigation. Neurobiologist Steven Hyman of Harvard University observes that "there is an incredible hunger to have tests to separate truth from deception, science be damned."[26]

Technical challenges include creating scans that distinguish between the normal anxiety of anyone subject to a criminal investigation and the (presumably different) anxiety of the person who is lying to investigators.[27] Also, the human brain processes information much more quickly than scans are currently able to measure. Practical factors may also be limiting. For an fMRI scan to proceed, the patient must remain relatively still inside a large, expensive, tubelike machine. Professor Wiseman notes, "It's not the sort of thing every police station has in the back, but in the future, potentially in high-profile cases, it might be something people want to look at."

The End of Interrogation?

How could brain scans impact mass incarceration and individual rights? Advances in fMRI research could mean the end of traditional police questioning of suspects. Professor Sean Thompson writes in the *Cornell Law Review*, "Torture is obsolete, or at least obsolescent. Researchers, funded by the Department of Defense, have developed technologies that may render the 'dark art' of interrogation unnecessary."[28]

Professor Thompson is principally concerned with interrogation and the "counterresistance techniques" employed not in the War on Drugs but rather in the War on Terror. As such, he characterizes fMRI research as a way of sidestepping the legal and public relations issues surrounding "aggressive" interrogation techniques. "The use of fMRI in the interrogation of these detainees would almost certainly not represent torture. Torture requires the infliction of pain; fMRI is painless."

The article notes that while fMRI is less physically invasive than many interrogation techniques, fMRI is "mentally invasive." Using fMRI technology "to extract information from a nonconsenting detainee would probably shock the conscience."[29] To illustrate this point, Professor Thompson describes potential uses of the fMRI scanner far beyond advanced lie detection. The Institute for Strategic Threat Analysis and Response (ISTAR), located at the University of Pennsylvania, has developed methods that apply fMRI to counterterrorism. For example, fMRI technology can already be used to determine if a subject recognizes a picture of another human face. "Seeing a familiar face stimulates brain activity in the hippocampus, which regulates memory and parts of the visual cortex," says Thompson. In addition, it may soon be possible to determine both the subject's level of familiarity with the face and the subject's feelings about the pictured individual. For example, researchers at the University of London believe they have located the specific brain regions associated with love. University of Pennsylvania scientist Daniel Engleben claims that within fifty years they "will have a way to essentially read minds."[30]

The Cornell article observes that most intelligence interrogation is about uncovering "tiny bits of truth" from a large number of detainees. For example, knowing that an individual has personally seen Osama bin Laden or a particular building in a city would have obvious intelligence value. Similar applications exist in everyday police work. Knowing which members of a criminal organization a suspect is acquainted with or whether the suspect has personally been to a crime scene would be invaluable to a police investigation.

While the article touts the technology as the end of torture, it admits that a certain level of coercion would be necessary to use the scan on unwilling subjects. "First, unlike blood tests, the fMRI scanner cannot operate on an unconscious individual, so some form of restraint will be required. Second, fMRI requires the subject to be very still during the procedure. Thus, the government will have to use considerable restraint to ensure that an unwilling subject remains virtually motionless." And, in the case of visual recognition technology, that he keeps his eyes open. . . .

The Future of Guilt

The future of criminal trials probably rests with forensic evidence such as that derived from instruments like the fMRI. While the technology has many temporary, and some inherent, limitations, the quest for a dependable lie detector is unstoppable. At best, fMRI scanners may do away with the worst excesses of interrogation and torture. At worst, though, fMRI may justify police and prosecutor abuses with the authoritative stamp of technology.

Reliable outcomes to criminal trials are, doubtless, a civic virtue. When we apprehend the actual culprit, there are obvious public safety benefits. Moreover, current police efforts to obtain statements from suspects are filled with trickery and deception at best, and threats and violence at worst. Brain scans promise a more direct route to the truth.

Still, the prospect of the government, and especially law enforcement agents, being able to read minds must give any citizen pause. People theoretically have a Fifth Amendment right to refuse a brain scan, but the Supreme Court could rule that scans are the kind of physical evidence (like blood or saliva samples) that is not protected by the privilege against self-incrimination. Like the E-Nose, brain scans, if they are truly reliable, offer more protection to the innocent than to the guilty. It is hard to anticipate their impact on incarceration. Certainly they would give prosecutors more bargaining power, which usually doesn't work out well for defendants. At the same time, they would offer more definitive proof of guilt—a boon for both public safety and falsely accused innocent people.

GENE THERAPY

Is there a criminal gene? Could we fix it to reduce incarceration? If we could, should we?

There is no one gene responsible for criminal behavior. There are, however, some genes that, when defective, seem to make people more prone to commit crimes. Gene therapy repairs those "broken" genes.[31] There are two major forms: somatic cell manipulation and germ-line therapy.[32] Somatic cell manipulation alters the nonreproductive cells in the human body,[33] while germ-line therapy alters the reproductive cells (i.e., sperm and egg).[34] Somatic therapy is intended to benefit the individual, while germ-line targets benefits for the individual's children.[35] With biological and technological advancement, both forms of gene therapy theoretically could be used to alter traits associated with criminality.[36]

Defective Genes

The MAOA (monoamine oxidase A) gene "directs the body to produce an enzyme that reduces the activity of a brain chemical called serotonin, which strongly influences mood."[37] There appears to be a link between the MAOA gene and antisocial behavior.[38] People (and animals) who lack MAOA display significantly higher signs of aggression and violence.[39] Low levels of the gene are correlated with attention-deficit disorder, depression, alcoholism, and learning disabilities.[40]

An important study reported in the journal *Science* found that 85 percent of a group of men who had been abused as children, and who also had low levels of MAOA, had committed crimes by age twenty-six.[41]

Impact on Mass Incarceration

Replacing or repairing defective MAOA genes can both reduce future incarceration and enhance public safety by curing people of a predisposition to violent criminal activity. Through genetic evaluation, people with MAOA deficiencies could be identified. With scientific advancements in gene therapy, the defective genes could be replaced with properly functioning genes.

The power to change criminal predispositions through gene therapy could revolutionize the criminal justice system. With the opportunity for treatment, offenders would have a better chance of permanent rehabilitation, which would justify their early release. And gene therapy techniques could be combined with other technological advances, such as GPS tracking, to create more flexible sentences for people convicted of crimes.[42]

Removing "criminal genes" would give individuals more control over their behavior, making them responsible, and culpable, for their actions. Those people with family histories of violence would no longer have to fear that they would continue the cycle. Parents would be able to eliminate any criminal predisposition in their children before they advance beyond the embryonic stage.[43] And individuals convicted of violent offenses would be less likely to recidivate after genetic treatment.

The problem, however, is whether the state should be in the business of encouraging—or requiring—people to change their genetic makeup. That's a very dangerous path, perhaps not so far from the eugenics practiced in Nazi Germany. The line, for example, between gene therapy, on one hand, and selective contraception and abortion, on the other hand, is not bright.

Science has, however, already started down the road, and there is probably no turning back. People will, in the near future, be modifying their genes and the genes of their children for all kinds of reasons—to prevent cancer, grow taller, change eye color, and increase IQ. If the coming generation of designer babies embodies interventions that enhance public safety and reduce mass incarceration, social justice advocates must give this technology serious consideration. As with drug detection devices and brain scans, the introduction of gene therapy in criminal justice is more a question of "when" than "if." Progressives can't stop the future, but they need to be prepared for the daunting challenge of making high-tech justice as consistent with human rights and civil liberties as possible.

9

The Beautiful Struggle:
Seven Ways to Take Back Justice

I want to end this book with good news. There are many things ordinary citizens can do, right now, to reclaim American justice.
This chapter recommends seven interventions that will make us
safer and more free. Some, like reducing the prison population by
500,000 and ending racial profiling, require the government to
act. I also suggest some other methods to reduce incarceration and
increase civil liberties that don't require any level of organization
beyond reaching out to a fellow citizen to offer a helping hand. If
you're not in a position to practice jury nullification, you can help
an at-risk young person graduate from high school. The point is
there is something that each of us can do. I hope I have made the
case for why we must.

1. PAY A KID TO FINISH HIGH SCHOOL

Children at risk of dropping out of high school should be paid to
graduate.

A study by the Rand Corporation compared various ways to prevent crime, including prison, "three strikes" laws, and social programs for both effectiveness and cost. The most effective way to
prevent crime was getting kids to graduate from high school by
using financial incentives. It worked far better than get-tough
criminal justice policies.[1] It was also the most cost effective of the
crime-prevention methods the study evaluated.[2]

According to the National Center for Education Statistics, America's high school graduation rate is about 88 percent.[3] Some researchers think that the actual rate is significantly lower. A 2004 study by the Harvard Civil Rights Project and the Urban Institute suggested that about 68 percent of children who enter the ninth grade graduate on time with a regular diploma. For African Americans, Latinos, and Native Americans, this figure is about 50 percent. We also know that at least 50 percent of people in prison don't have high school degrees.

Los Angeles County sheriff Lee Baca describes the high dropout rate in certain communities as a major public safety threat. He and other California law enforcement officials released a study that demonstrated that increasing graduation rates by 10 percent lowers homicide and assault rates by 20 percent, and would prevent 500 murders and 20,000 aggravated assaults in California every year.[4] Sheriff Baca stated, "We can't arrest our way out of the crime problem, but we can educate our way to a safer community."[5] The idea of paying children to graduate may seem odd, but the study found that graduation incentives could bring as much as a 15 percent overall reduction in crime.[6]

Studies suggest that teenagers respond to financial incentives just as well as adults do. The best evidence so far comes from the Quantum Opportunity Program (QOP). This program ran from 1995 until 2001, and implemented the financial incentives recommended in the Rand study as well as other early intervention measures.[7] "The QOP demonstration, funded by the U.S. Department of Labor and the Ford Foundation, was conducted in seven locations: Memphis; Cleveland; Washington, DC; Fort Worth; Houston; Philadelphia; and Yakima, Washington."[8]

In all jurisdictions, graduation rates increased. According to the National Council of Juvenile and Family Court Judges, the QOP program was successful because it "starts early before many young people are in deep trouble."[9] In Philadelphia, 76 percent of students graduated and moved on to postsecondary education.[10] Further, after two years of the program, those students who had been involved accounted for half the number of arrests of the control group, who did not participate.[11]

Atlanta now employs a "Learn and Earn" program in which students are paid $8 an hour to attend after-school tutoring.[12] Baltimore has a similar program, paying students who improve their scores on state graduation exams.[13] While neither of these programs directly pays students to graduate, they do show an effort to use innovative means to encourage graduation.

Discomfort with the idea of paying kids to go to school seems palpable. The California assembly passed the "Preventing Crime Through Graduation Incentives Pilot Project."[14] This program was designed to implement the RAND study, including the financial incentives for graduation. The state senate refused to allow it to come up for a vote.

It's true, ideally, that we should not have to pay children to go to school. But the world is far from ideal, and high school dropouts get the rawest end of the stick. On every measure of achievement and success, they are at the bottom. Maybe this would be tolerable as the consequences of their own bad choices if the entire community didn't also suffer. The fact is, however, that everyone pays for that choice, and some crime victims pay with their money or their lives.

So some communities are getting off their high horses in the name of safety and positive outcomes for kids. At Chelsea High School outside Boston, students with perfect attendance get $100 a year—set aside in an account until they graduate.[15] In New York City, Mayor Michael Bloomberg proposed cash payments of between $50 and $1,500 to encourage kids to stay in school. It turns out it's not that expensive to pay off a kid. The rewards society reaps, however, are immeasurable.

2. TAKE IT TO THE COURTHOUSE

You can work with other people in your community to educate citizens, especially potential jurors, about the social and economic costs of mass incarceration. Every American needs to understand that the United States would be safer and more free if it did not have some of the toughest sentences—and the highest rate of incarceration—in the world.

As Chapter 4 explains, the Constitution provides jurors with a unique power—jury nullification—to protest prosecutorial over-reaching and excessive punishment. Most jurors don't know they have this ability, but you can inform them. You should not approach jurors in individual cases, but you can talk to potential jurors in community organizations, political gatherings, unions, and at places of worship and cultural events. You can write letters to the editor, posts on blogs, create informational videos on YouTube, and even pass out pamphlets, in the grand old American tradition.

The goal is for every citizen to understand that when they sit as jurors, they don't have to tolerate the lock-'em-up mentality of our dysfunctional criminal justice system. The jury system is designed to be a check on law enforcement. If prosecutors are exercising their power in a fair way, as they do when they go after violent criminals, they have nothing to worry about. Nullification—when the jury unanimously agrees that even if the accused person is guilty, he should not be punished—will only happen when law enforcement goes too far. History has shown that strategic nullification can work just as the framers of the Constitution intended—as an appropriate and effective way to improve U.S. justice.

Go to JurorsforJustice.com to connect with other concerned citizens in your community and learn more about strategic jury nullification.

3. GET THE LEAD OUT

In 1994, the economist Richard Nevin discovered a startling correlation between the violent-crime rate and the lead in gasoline. When Nevin compared leaded gas consumption with FBI crime statistics, he found an almost perfect correspondence: as lead gas use climbed and then fell, so did the rate of violent crime.

What does lead have to do with crime? It's long been known that lead is neurotoxic and particularly harmful to the developing nervous systems of young children.[16] Extremely high blood lead levels can cause severe neurologic problems, and even death.

It's the low to moderate exposure that's the most insidious. Among adults, symptoms of lead poisoning include weakness, excessive fatigue, irritability, infertility, and reduced sex drive.[17] In children, lead exposure can also lead to both learning and behavioral disorders. Lead absorption is linked to lower IQs, reduced physical stature and growth, impaired hearing, reduced attention span, hyperactivity, and behavioral problems. Significant for its relationship to violent crime, lead poisoning results in higher aggression and a reduction in impulse control.

Several decades ago, the greatest source of contamination was leaded gas. The Clean Air Act of 1970 solved this problem; between 1975 and 1985 lead was virtually eliminated from gasoline. Since states kept excellent records of both the amount of lead in their gasoline and crime rates, scholars were curious to see whether there would be a correlation between the two. Our prime years for committing violent crimes are our teens and early twenties. The premise was that young children exposed to lead in the 1970s (from gas exhaust fumes, lead paint, and contaminated household dust) would be expected to have higher rates of criminality when they reached this time in their lives, whereas children born after lead was phased out of gas would be expected to have lower rates. Reports thus far have shown this to be the case.

Professor Nevin thinks that lead poisoning is the biggest factor behind violent crime.[18] A bunch of criminologists have offered explanations about why crime spiked in the late 1980s and then fell, quite precipitously. New York City, for example, had fewer than 500 homicides in 2007. That's the lowest number since at least 1963, when the NYPD began keeping accurate records. But crime has fallen virtually everywhere, not just in New York City. The decline is very different from what criminologists had predicted in the early 1980s. There's been a cottage industry of explanations. The most sensational, popularized in the bestseller *Freakonomics*, is that the legalization of abortion in the early 1970s prevented a class of criminals from being born who would have wreaked havoc when they reached their prime crime-committing years.

Other theories about why violent crime has declined have considered demographics, economic conditions, police strategies, and even the idea that crack dealers—responsible for many homicides in the late 1980s—learned to play nicer. As chapter 2 explained, the fact that so many people starting going to prison for long periods of time gets some of the credit for the early drop. But criminologists credit no more than 20 percent of the decline to the higher rate of incarceration. Indeed, "the tipping point" analysis suggests that crime rates would be even lower than they are now if so many people were not incarcerated.

Now we know. The most important explanation is environmental. It's lead. Professor Levin's genius was to compare data from nine countries. These countries had various levels of incarceration rates, abortion laws, police strategies, and demographic configurations. In all nine countries, the strongest predictor of the rise and fall of violent crime was the amount of lead to which children were exposed.

The most comprehensive study has been done by Jessica Reyes, an economist at Amherst College. She compared lead exposure and crime rates in all fifty states and the District of Columbia. She discovered that "childhood lead exposure can increase the likelihood of violent criminal behavior, and that this effect is large enough to affect national crime trends significantly. The fact that leaded gas is relatively rare now predicts continuing declines in the future." [19]

Other scholars have found the same results. Unfortunately many children still grow up with significant exposure to lead from sources other than gasoline, including paint, dust, and contaminated soil. One study, conducted in 2001, reported that counties in the U.S. study with high lead levels had murder rates four times that of counties with low lead levels."[20] Another study found that teenagers arrested in Pittsburgh had lead levels four times higher than teens who hadn't been arrested.[21] A different study of data from 129 U.S. cities reached the preliminary conclusion that communities with a larger percentage of children with high levels of lead in their blood are "significantly more likely" to have higher rates of violent crime.[22]

Ultimately, the most effective way of reducing lead poisoning is to prevent exposure. According to Mary Jean Brown, chief of the Lead Poisoning Prevention Branch of the Centers for Disease Control, "Childhood lead poisoning is a completely preventable illness. We know what the causes are, how children get it, and how to prevent it. Essentially, the way to prevent it is to control or eliminate sources of lead in the environment and around children."

Federal law on lead poisoning is surprisingly weak, given the high stakes. The regulations that provide relief to children require that they actually be poisoned before the government will step in to help. Since lead poisoning is easy to prevent but difficult to treat, this limitation renders the law much less effective, especially in terms of preventing crime.

Massachusetts has one of the best state laws. It requires inspection of lead levels in homes in two situations—a request by any occupant, or when the state is informed of a case of lead poisoning. When a lead poisoning case is the cause, the director may inspect both the victim's current premises and any premise the victim resided in during the previous twelve months. The legislation mandates a program for the early detection of lead poisoning, including screening all children under the age of six. The law allows for strong enforcement, including fines for people who use lead paint.

By comparison, Rhode Island has few laws pertaining to leaded paints. Children there demonstrate significantly higher rates of lead poisoning than those in their neighboring state.[23] The federal government, and the other states, should enact laws based on those in Massachusetts. It is one of the best things that we can do for homeland security. It will prevent crime, it will prevent incarceration, and, most important, it will save lives.

4. "HUG A THUG"

How's this for a way to reduce incarceration? The police know you committed a crime, but they don't arrest you right away. Instead they call your mother. Police in High Point, North Carolina, used this kind of strategy to get drugs off the street and reduce incarceration. It worked. The big idea, as developed by criminologist David Kennedy, was to ask the community to intervene in place of the police. The goals, according to Kennedy, were to "permanently eliminate overt drug markets (street sales, drug houses, and the like); reduce the violent crime and disorder associated with those markets; reduce incarceration and other harmful effects of law enforcement; and heal the rift between law enforcement and the minority communities in which overt markets are found."[24]

The program in High Point began after the police department consulted Kennedy, who's a professor at the John Jay College of Criminal Justice in New York City. The High Point Police Department decided to focus on a four-block area known as the West End because, in addition to the drug activity, there had been a number of homicides in the area, and there was also a strong community-level network.[25]

The first step in "The West End Project," as it came to be known, was for police to gather intelligence identifying key players in the neighborhood's drug activity. Of the twenty-six they identified, six were taken into custody immediately based on other crimes and their potential threat to their community. Police developed strong criminal cases against the twenty other offenders, but they did not arrest them. Once the cops had gathered all the information they needed, they went to the community. The plan was to keep those twenty men out of prison and to improve community safety at the same time.

First, the police department presented the idea to an influential neighborhood organization to get its support. Then, in what was probably the most important step, they visited the bad dudes' moms. Actually, the "influential" they consulted for each offender could have been any family member, but in most cases it was the mother. Each visit was held in a neutral location, like a church, and included a police officer, a community member, and a minister. During the visit the police officer explained the program to the family member and produced an unsigned arrest warrant that would be executed if the offender didn't straighten up. Finally, a rally was held to "reclaim" the neighborhood and demonstrate that the community was no longer going to tolerate drug activity.[26]

The next part of the program was called the "notification." Offenders who wanted to avoid going to jail attended this meeting, along with a wide cross-section of the community (including ministers, city council members, resource coordinators, federal public defenders, and volunteers). The offenders were led to a large room along with police and judicial officials. The room displayed photos of the major drug houses and the offenders who had been arrested the day before. There were also large binders full of information about the criminal cases the police had developed against them.

The police explained that the community would no longer tolerate drug activity. They also advised of the social services available to the offenders for their fresh start. The session ended with the chief of police telling the offenders, "I'm pulling for you."

The program resulted in a dramatic decrease in drug and violent crime. The most significant changes, however, were in the community dynamics and in the lives of the offenders. Members of the community reported feeling safer in the neighborhood, and a network of partnerships developed between community organizations and the police department. There has been a 36 percent decrease in crime in the area.[27]

High Point chief of police James Fealy said, "It produces results that are so dramatic it's almost incredible. It is sustainable. It does not produce the community harms that our traditional street-sweeping, unfocused efforts have."

So the police reduced crime by *not* locking people up. Instead cops made neighborhoods safer by caring about offenders and getting the entire community to root that the bad guys would turn into good guys. And most of them did. It's a story heartwarming enough to make a thug cry. The U.S. Justice Department is now funding similar programs across the country.

5. END RACIAL PROFILING

I live in the District of Columbia, in a middle-class, racially integrated neighborhood. One day, as I walked near my home, I was stopped by the police and questioned about where I live. After protesting the interrogation—one does not have to reside in a place to walk on the public streets—I reluctantly showed the police my home. My word, alas, was not good enough; the police requested proof that I lived there. I refused to display such proof. The police—five officers—refused to leave until I did. The encounter lasted approximately one hour. It ended when one officer interviewed my neighbor, who confirmed my residence.[28]

The police claimed that they stopped me because they do not often see people walking in my neighborhood. I believe that I was stopped because I am black. The officers also were African American, a fact that does not for me weaken the racial explanation. If I am right, however—if my blackness was the reason the officers found me suspicious—the police actually acted lawfully. Most courts allow the police to use race-dependent assessments of suspicion.

Episodes like this are so well known that when I wanted to write about it for a legal magazine, my editor told me that the story would be part of a "genre." The victims of "driving while black" profiling often seem sympathetic, and in the stories that become part of the "genre," they are innocent. There was a time when the battle to end racial profiling seemed to be gaining currency, based in part on the power of the rhetoric. Bills were proposed in Congress, and some local police departments began collecting data as a first step to ending the practice.

Then came the terrible morning of September 11, 2001. Afterward, it seemed to some people only common sense that airport security officers should pay more attention to Arabs and Muslims. After all, the argument went, all of the 9/11 hijackers were Arabs.

There are now four different points of view on the value of profiling:

1. It's reasonable for law enforcement to use race as one factor in deciding who's suspicious. Just because you're white and driving through a low-income African American neighborhood at 2 A.M. doesn't necessarily mean that you are looking for drugs, but the police are just doing their job when they keep a closer eye on you.

2. It's unreasonable for law enforcement to use race as a factor. We are less safe when TSA agents pay closer attention to Arabs because anyone planning to blow up an airplane now would have the good sense to avoid looking like the profile.

3. It's reasonable for law enforcement to consider race, but officers still should not do so because it's un-American. In the United States people should be judged by the content of their character—even when there might be some rationality to a racial consideration.

4. It's reasonable for law enforcement to profile for national security because the potential benefit—preventing a terrorist attack—is so great. It's unreasonable in the "driving while black" cases because the cost is so high and the benefit— finding drugs—is relatively minimal.

All of these claims have vocal supporters, but sometimes not along the political ideology that you might expect. The liberal

Massachusetts congressman Barney Frank, for example, supports position 4. He says that "pulling over some black kid because he's driving" is a "terrible intrusion." Airports, however, call for a different approach: "[N]ational origin would be a part of it. . . . In certain countries, people are angrier at us than elsewhere." Frank describes the intrusion at the airport as "incremental," and says, "If no harm is being done, and you're not being in any way disadvantaged, I am reluctant to think that there's any great problem."[29]

The congressman incorrectly calculates both the cost and benefit of profiling. As someone who has been the victim of profiling more times than I care to remember, I have an acute appreciation of the pain. You know it's not your fault, you tell yourself it doesn't have anything to do with you, but it's still corrosive. To say that it can plant the seeds of hate isn't going too far.

The benefit, however, is either marginal or nonexistent. In the "driving while black" context, there is the obviously self-fulfilling prophecy aspect. The police think that African Americans are more likely to have drugs and, accordingly, they stop and search them more frequently. There is a close relationship between looking for things and finding things. If the police decided that law professors were criminally prone, and focused more on them, the number of my colleagues in the criminal justice system would precipitiously increase.

In the charged context of national security, it is precisely because the stakes are so high that profiling is irrational. For example, recently the Middle East has seen a rash of terrorist attacks—by female terrorists. They apparently don't receive the same scrutiny as male terrorists.

Likewise, a few years ago, when ten people were killed in DC from random gunshots, all everyone talked about was who the sniper might be. "Some crazy white boy," I predicted to my colleague. My profile was unscientific, but a brother committing that kind of crime didn't fit in my schema. All I can say now, after an African American man and boy were convicted of those attacks, is that I am glad I didn't run into those "brothers" during that terrifying October. My false sense of security could have gotten me killed.

Ultimately, that's the problem with racial profiling. It makes us feel more secure when we are not. It's one of the main factors responsible for the gross racial disparities in prison. When law enforcement stops using race to gauge suspicion, and starts using behavior, we will be safer, our prisons will not not be as segregated, and our nation will be closer to the grand and egalitarian ideals that our Constitution professes.

6. MAKE PUNISHMENT FIT THE CRIME

One important explanation for mass incarceration is the incredibly long sentences that U.S. inmates currently serve. By any measure — compared to thirty years ago in the United States, or now in Europe — American prisoners serve outsized sentences. "Unlocking America: Why and How to Reduce America's Prison Population," a comprehensive study by criminal justice experts, found that "for the same crimes, American prisoners receive sentences twice as long as English prisoners, three times as long as Canadian prisoners, four times as long as Dutch prisoners, five to ten times as long as French prisoners, and five times as long as Swedish prisoners. Yet these countries' rates of violent crime are lower than ours, and their rates of property crime are comparable." [30]

American punishment simply does not fit the crime. Consider the following cases:

- Weldon Angelos was sentenced to fifty-five years in prison for three counts of selling marijuana while being in the presence of a weapon (he never showed or used the gun). He was twenty-five years old at the time of his sentencing and had only one prior offense, for which he had received three months. Angelos's projected release date is October 2, 2051.
- Jessica Hall is a stay-at-home mom with three children.

While her husband was serving with the marines in Iraq, she had a moment of road rage. She threw a cup of McDonald's coffee at another car that had cut her off. She was charged with "throwing a missile at an occupied vehicle" and sentenced to two years in prison.[31]

- Elisa Kelly and George Robinson, a married couple, hosted a party for their son and nine of his friends. They allowed underage drinking at the party and were sentenced to eight years in prison. Later the sentence was reduced to twenty-seven months.[32]

This kind of punishment is the result of the dysfunctional politics of American criminal justice. Elected lawmakers establish the sentences, and judges, who are elected in most states, impose them. Most are afraid to look "soft on crime." The people who suffer are usually poor, and often racial minorities; they lack political clout even without a criminal conviction.

Many states, and the U.S. Congress, have established "sentencing commissions" to recommend appropriate punishment. These commissions, which include community members and criminal justice experts, provide a degree of political insulation for judges and lawmakers. If someone attacks them for a punishment that seems too low, they can say that they were "just listening to the experts." At a minimum, recommendations from sentencing commissions should be carefully considered. This doesn't always happen now. The U.S. Congress, for example, has refused to assent to the U.S. Sentencing Commission's recommendation to equalize disparities in cocaine sentences that have racially disparate effects.

Citizens have to be aware of all the consequences of mass incarceration, including the "tipping point" where incarceration increases crime. Unduly harsh sentences lead only to distrust of criminal justice and disrespect for law.

7. FREE 500,000 AMERICANS

Why should we support release for many of the 500,000 people who are now locked up for nonviolent, victimless crimes? As I hope I have demonstrated by now: to make us all safer and more free. How do we let 500,000 people out of prison? Carefully.

There is a way. Several prison systems have reduced their prison population and seen crime go down at the same time.

Some states have been forced to release inmates early for financial reasons or because of overcrowded prison conditions. In 2008 a federal court recommended that California release 40,000 inmates over a four-year period because of prison overcrowding (this would put the state prison system at "just" 152 percent over designed capacity). The court suggested that parole violators and some nonviolent offenders be diverted to community treatment or alternative-punishment programs. California governor Arnold Schwarzenegger also has proposed releasing 22,000 low-risk inmates early in the wake of budget deficit problems.[33] The state's prison budget is $10 billion a year, and the 70 percent offender recidivism rate is costing California a substantial amount.[34] The plan would save an estimated $260 million.[35]

Under the governor's plan, low-risk (i.e., nonviolent) inmates with fewer than two years left to serve would be considered for early release.[36] The majority of inmates eligible are expected to be drug offenders, and the remaining eligible inmates are likely serving sentences for property offenses (e.g., forgery, car theft, etc.).[37]

Virtually every recommendation for reducing incarceration has three components: first, reducing the use of prison for nonviolent offenders, especially people convicted of drug offenses; second, ending the practice of reincarcerating people for technical parole or probation violations (such as failing to get a job, not paying supervision fees, or not attending drug treatment programs); and third, reducing the term of parole and probation periods after inmates have served their time.

One study reports that if these three reforms were implemented, the prison population would be cut in half, with no detriment to public safety, and considerable savings to taxpayers.[38] Many of these measures have begun in some American jurisdictions (possession of small amounts of drugs is de facto decriminalized in twelve states, and many cities), again with no cost to public safety.

CONCLUSION

As I finish this book, the United States recently has elected as president Barack Obama, a brilliant man who used marijuana and cocaine during high school and college and got away with it. If his "criminality" had been handled like that of the 500,000 people now locked up for nonviolent drug offenses, it is doubtful that he would have become the most powerful person in the world. An important question now is: Will President Obama use his power to help other people who made mistakes, especially those who committed drug crimes like his? Dare the 2.3 million prisoners in the United States have the audacity of hope?

Obama told a college audience in 2004 that "the war on drugs has been a failure."[39] During his presidential campaign, he supported decriminalizing marijuana. He also seemed critical, as I have been, of incarceration for nonviolent drug crimes. In a 2007 speech at Howard University, Obama said, "We will review [drug] sentences to see where we could be smarter on crime and reduce the blind and counterproductive warehousing of nonviolent offenders."[40]

In the heat of the campaign, however, Obama seemed to retreat. The conservative *Washington Times* newspaper posted a video of Obama's 2004 speech on its Web site.[41] In response, Obama's spokesperson first said that the story was old news because Obama "had always" supported decriminalization.[42] The spokesman reversed himself the next day, saying that Obama did not support decriminalization and that "if you're convicted of a crime, you should be punished." The spokesperson did, however, reiterate Obama's concern about long sentences for nonviolent drug offenses.[43]

The lesson is that Obama, the master politician, is susceptible to the dysfunctional politics of criminal justice. He isn't the first. Another master politician, Bill Clinton, told *Rolling Stone* in 2000 that "we really need an examination of our entire prison policy."[44] Yet more Americans were locked up during Clinton's presidency than any other administration in the country's history. Barack Obama is smart, his heart is in the right place, and he cares about the hundreds of thousands of Americans who are incarcerated for nonviolent drug offenses. With two wars and a crumbling economy, however, he probably will not be sufficiently motivated to create the fundamental change our criminal justice system needs, unless "we the people" demand it.

We must insist that our government reduce the number of Americans behind bars by at least 500,000. This can be accomplished, in part, by making prison sentences shorter and ending jail time for technical violations of probation and parole. We should also greatly expand the use of alternatives to incarceration including home confinement and make sure that those alternatives are available to all eligible persons, regardless of income.

The most effective way to reduce incarceration, though, would be to stop sending nonviolent drug offenders to prison. President Obama's inspiring life story disproves many of the suppositions of the war on drugs, including that drug use is immoral, that users — especially cocaine users — inevitably become addicts and thieves, and that criminal justice is the appropriate response to drug use. Arrest, prosecution, and punishment have as much potential to be as counterproductive to the average drug consumer as they would have been to young Barack Obama.

Strategic jury nullification sends the urgent message that "we the people" agree with President Obama: locking up nonviolent offenders is "blind and counterproductive." We need change right now. Jurors have the power to make effective criminal justice a top priority of state and federal lawmakers and prosecutors. Martin Luther King jurors are not likely to be received any more warmly by the powers-that-be than were the civil rights protestors of the 1950s and 1960s, but they have the same potential to create fundamental change, and one day may be regarded in the same heroic light as champions of freedom like Rosa Parks and Congressman John Lewis.

Judges must be willing to clamp down on the ever-widening power of the police. Each judge, whether she hears cases in a municipal criminal court or in the U.S. Supreme Court, must uphold the Constitution by protecting citizens from arbitrary and coercive police practices. Americans now have fewer civil liberties with each passing Supreme Court term, and, in the long run, this represents as much of a threat to our freedom as mass incarceration.

Law enforcement must end its overdependence on snitches. Simply put, reliable criminal justice does not exist when police and prosecutors pay off witnesses. Promising criminals money or a break from prosecution in their own cases if they help make a case against somebody else is as destructive to public safety as it is to neighborly values. Communities teeming with informants and citizen-spies are un-American in the most fundamental sense.

We need to listen, thoughtfully, to hip-hop. No other aspect of our culture has considered as carefully, and as personally, the costs and benefits of the American punishment regime. Since members of the hip-hop nation, who often come from the most dangerous communities, have more of a vested interest in safety than most other Americans, they help us understand that treating people who have messed up with love and dignity is, for law-abiding citizens, an act of self-interest and community safety.

Clarence Thomas, the conservative African American Supreme Court justice, said that earlier in his career when he was a judge in DC, every day he looked out of the window of his office, saw all the young black men filing into criminal court in chains, and thought, "There, but for the grace of God, go I."[45] The determination of who goes to criminal court in chains should not be so fortuitous. It should not depend so much on class and race. As long as it does, a responsibility of good citizenship includes agitating for justice for all. We can "get free," but like every great movement for human rights, this beautiful struggle requires diligence and courage.* The future of freedom in the United States demands nothing less.

---

* *The Beautiful Struggle* is the title of the hip-hop artist Talib Kweli's second album (Rawkus/Geffen, 2004). It comes from a speech by Martin Luther King Jr. in which he said, "We must move past indecision to action. Now let us begin. Now let us rededicate ourselves to the long and bitter, but beautiful, struggle for a new world." "Beyond Vietnam," address delivered to the Clergy and Laymen Concerned about Vietnam at Riverside Church, New York, April 4, 1967, http://stanford.edu/group/King/publications/speeches/Beyond_Vietnam.pdf.

NOTES

1. The Hunter Gets Captured by the Game:
A Prosecutor Meets American Criminal Justice

1. What follows is not a word-for-word account of my arrest, prosecution, and trial but rather a description based on my recollections, contemporaneous notes, and interviews with witnesses and trial observers. The quotes are not necessarily verbatim but intended to represent the substance of the statements and testimony at trial. All of the names, dates, and facts are accurate to the best of my ability.

2. Attractiveness has been found to be a biasing factor in juror decisions (along with race, gender and occupational status). Attractive defendants are less likely to be convicted by mock jurors. David Landy and Elliot Aronson, "The Influence of the Character of the Criminal and His Victim on the Decisions of Simulated Jurors," *Journal of Experimental Social Psychology* 5 (1969): 141, 146–51. Mock jurors are also more likely to give harsher sentences to defendants when shown pictures of defendants categorized as unattractive. David B. Gray and Richard D. Ashmore, "Biasing Influence of Defendants' Characteristics on Simulated Sentencing," *Psychological Reports* 38 (1976): 727–36. Similarly, attractive plaintiffs in civil suits have been found to be more likely to win and collect more money. Cookie Stephan and Judy Corder Tully, "The Influence of Physical Attractiveness of a Plaintiff on the Decisions of Simulated Jurors," *Journal of Social Psychology* 101 (1977): 149.

3. Federal Bureau of Investigation, *Crime in the United States, 2006,* http://www.fbi.gov/ucr/cius2006/.

2. Safety First: Why Mass Incarceration Matters

1. Allison Klein, "D.C. Police to Check Drivers in Violence-Plagued Trinidad," *Washington Post,* June 5, 2008, A01.

2. As of June 30, 2007, there were 2,299,116 prisoners being held in federal or state prisons or in local jails. This is a 1.8 percent total increase from year-end 2006. U.S. Department of Justice, Bureau of Justice Statistics, "Prison Statistics," http://www.ojp.usdoj.gov/bjs/prisons.htm.

3. The approximate number of people imprisoned in the world is 9 million. The United States imprisons 2.25 million of them, which is 25 percent. Roy Walmsley, *World Prison Population List*, 6th ed. (London: King's College International Centre for Prison Studies, 2007). The United States comprises 4.5 percent of the world's population. U.S. Central Intelligence Agency, *The World Factbook* (Washington, DC: 2007).

4. Ed Burns, "Undercover, Unreliable and Unaddressed: Reconsidering the Use of Informants in Drug Law Enforcement," American Civil Liberties Union, roundtable discussion transcript, Atlanta, GA, May 15, 2007, 11.

5. Eric Schlosser, "The World: Up in Smoke; the U.S. Bucks a Trend on Marijuana Laws," *New York Times*, June 1, 2003, http://query.nytimes.com/gst/full page.html?res=9F06E0D131430F932A35755C0A9659C8B63.

6. Glen Ford, *Racism: The Growth Engine of the American Prison Gulag* (Washington, DC: Pew Charitable Trust, 2007). Pew Charitable Trust fifty-state study cited ibid.

7. By the 1990s the United States was opening on average one new prison per week. Justice Policy Institute, http://justicepolicyinstitute.org.

8. The U.S. Supreme Court upheld an Iowa law which allows someone to be arrested and taken before a magistrate judge immediately for a traffic violation even if incarceration is not permitted as a sentence for that offense. *Knowles v. Iowa*, 525 U.S. 113, 115 (1998).

9. It was reasonable for the officer to take the action he did (forcing the car down the incline) in order to protect bystanders from the respondent, "who intentionally placed himself and the public in danger by unlawfully engaging in the reckless, high-speed flight." *Scott v. Harris*, 127 S. Ct. 1769, 1778 (2007).

10. High crime is a relevant contextual consideration in the *Terry* analysis. In addition, nervous, evasive behavior is a pertinent factor in determining whether an officer has reasonable suspicion to stop someone. Flight from officers is suggestive of nervousness. *Illinois v. Wardlow*, 528 U.S. 119, 124 (2000).

11. The court holds that the traditional definition of "voluntariness" does not require proof of knowledge of a right to refuse as the sine qua non of an effective consent to a search. *Schneckloth v. Bustamonte*, 412 U.S. 218, 234 (1973).

12. The officer's probable cause to believe petitioners violated the traffic code rendered the stop reasonable and the evidence seized admissible. *Whren v. United States*, 517 U.S. 806, 817 (1996).

13. David A. Harris, *Profiles in Injustice: Why Racial Profiling Cannot Work* (New York: The New Press, 2005). Also Randall Kennedy, *Race, Crime and the Law* (New York: Pantheon, 1997), 136–67.

14. The most recent release statistics state that 713,473 prisoners were released in 2006, up 2.1 percent from 2005. U.S. Department of Justice, Bureau of Statistics, "Prison Inmates at Midyear 2007," June 2008, http://www.ojp.usdoj.gov/bjs/pub/ascii/pim07.txt. As of 1994, approximately two-thirds (67.5 percent) were re-arrested within three years. U.S. Department of Justice, Bureau of Justice Statistics, "In a 15 State Study, Over Two-thirds of Released Prisoners Were Rearrested in Three Years," July 7, 2007, http://www.ojp.usdoj.gov/bjs/reentry/recidivism.htm. At least 95 percent of all state prisoners will be released at some point. U.S.

Department of Justice, Bureau of Justice Statistics, "Reentry Trends in the United States," July 7, 2007, http://www.ojp.usdoj.gov/bjs/reentry/reentry.htm. The statistics I found for substance abuse were very different: 56 percent of state and 50 percent of federal prisoners had a substance abuse problem; 40 percent of state and 49 percent of federal prisoners with drug problems received treatment while in prison; http://www.ojp.usdoj.gov/bjs/pub/pdf/dudsfp04.pdf.

15. Michael Jacobson, *Downsizing Prisons: How to Reduce Crime and End Mass Incarceration* (New York: New York University Press, 2005), 128.

16. Jim Holt, "The Way We Live Now: 8-15-04: Idea Lab—Decarcerate?" *New York Times*, August 15, 2004, http://query.nytimes.com/gst/fullpage.html?res=9F01E7D91F3CF936A2575BC0A9629C8B63.

17. Raymond V. Liedka et al., "The Crime Control Effect of Incarceration: Does Scale Matter?" *Crime and Public Policy* 5, no. 2 (2006): 245–48.

18. The most prevalent theory for an increase in crime as a result of incarceration is that of social disorganization. The social disorganization theory in relation to public safety ultimately suggests that social cohesion in the community has the effect of reducing crime. Incarceration destroys social cohesion in many different ways, which ultimately causes the crime rate to go up. Todd R. Clear et al., "Coercive Mobility and Crime: A Preliminary Examination of Concentrated Incarceration and Social Disorganization," *Justice Quarterly* 20, no. 1 (2003): 35. Many researchers cite the social disorganization theory as a reason that incarceration does not effectively reduce the crime rate and often increases it. This theory has been proven more specifically through research into smaller populations. See Eric Lotke and Jason Ziedenberg, "Tipping Point: Maryland's Overuse of Incarceration, and the Impact on Community Safety," *Justice Policy Institute* (2005): 15; *Tomishu v. Kovandzic* and John J. Sloan, "Police Levels and Crime Rates Revisited: A County Level Analysis from Florida (1980–1998)," *Journal of Criminal Justice* 30 (2002): 65–73.

19. Marc Mauer, "Thinking About Prison and Its Impact in the Twenty-First Century," *Ohio State Journal of Criminal Law* 2 (2005): 607, 613.

20. Donald Braman, *Doing Time on the Outside: Incarceration and Family Life in Urban America* (Ann Arbor: University of Michigan Press, 2007).

21. The most recent statistics (August 2000) show that 54.7 percent of men in state prison and 63.4 percent of men in federal prison had a minor child. For women, 65.3 percent in state prison and 58.8 percent in federal prison had a minor child. Christopher J. Mumola, *Special Report: Incarcerated Parents and Their Children*, U.S. Department of Justice, Bureau of Justice Statistics, August 2000, http://ojp.usdoj.gov/bjs/pub/pdf/iptc.pdf.

22. Children of prisoners are seven times more likely to become involved with the juvenile or adult criminal justice systems than their peers. U.S. Department of Health and Human Services, Administration for Children and Families, Family Youth Services Bureau, *Report to Congress: The Mentoring Children of Prisoners Project*, 2007, http://www.acf.hhs.gov/programs/fysb/content/docs/07_mcpreport.htm.

23. Even when given an explanation of one's criminal history, fast food chains are reluctant to hire convicted felons. Claudia Rowe, "For Teen Felons, Hardest

Job Is Finding Honest Work," *Seattle Post-Intelligencer*, February 22, 2008. The threat of a lawsuit could be one of the reasons they are resistant to hire convicted felons. "Parents Sue McDonald's Over Hiring of Felon as Manager," *Nation's Restaurant News*, August 12, 2002.

24. John Gibbons and Nicholas Katzenbach, *Confronting Confinement: A Report on the Commission on Safety and Abuse in American Prisons*, 2006, 84, http://www.prisoncommission.org/report.asp.

25. The overall crime rates in European countries are not that different from those in the United States. The differences in crime rates between the United States and other countries can be attributed to our defining more behavior as criminal. In fact, the United States has a relatively low incidence of property crimes in comparison to Europe. Adam Liptak, "American Exception: Inmate Count in U.S. Dwarfs Other Nations," *New York Times*, April 23, 2008.

26. However, the rates of violent crimes in the United States are disproportionate to those in France and Germany. The U.S. murder rate is 5.7 per 100,000 people, compared to 3.9 and 3.4, respectively, in France and Germany. The U.S. rape rate is 30.9 per 100,000, compared to 17 and 11 in France and Germany. Federal Bureau of Investigation, "Crime Rates in the United States 1986–2006," *Crime in the United States 2006*, July 10, 2008, http://www.fbi.gov/ucr/cius2006/data/table _01.html; *European Sourcebook of Crime and Criminal Justice*, July 10, 2008, http://www.europeansourcebook.org.

27. Spending for the 2007–2008 fiscal year for prisons in California will be approximately $10 billion (up 9 percent from the previous year). Spending for higher education will be $12 billion (up 6 percent from the previous year). If spending continues to grow at these rates, by the 2012–2013 fiscal year, more money will be spent on prisons than on higher education in California (with prisons at $15.4 billion and higher education at $15.3 billion). James Sterngold, "Prisons Budget to Trump Colleges," *San Francisco Chronicle*, May 21, 2007, A1, http://www.sfgate.com/cgi-bin/article.cgi?file=/c/a/2007/05/21/MNG4KPUKV 51.DTL.

28. Vermont, Michigan, Oregon, Connecticut, and Delaware all spend either the same or more on prisons than on higher education. All five of these states spend between $1.00 and $1.37 on prisons versus $1.00 spent on education. "One in 100: Behind Bars in America 2008," Pew Charitable Trust, http://www.pew centeronthestates.org/report_detail.aspx?id=33428,16.

29. James Sterngold, "Prisons Budget to Trump Colleges," *San Francisco Chronicle*, May 21, 2007, http://www.sfgate.com/cgi-bin/article.cgi?file=/c/a/ 2007/05/21/MNG4KPUKV51.DTL.

30. Russia's rate of incarceration is 611 per 100,000, compared to the United States' rate of 735 per 100,000. Walmsley, *World Prison Population List*.

31. The incarceration rate in the United States is five times as high as the next highest Western nation. David Cole, "As Freedom Advances: The Paradox of Severity in American Criminal Justice," *University of Pennsylvania Journal of Constitutional Law* 3 (2001): 457.

32. Robert J. MacCoun and Peter Reuter, *Drug War Heresies: Learning from Other Vices, Times and Places* (New York: Cambridge University Press, 2001), 24.

33. "The risk of unrestrained state authorities, or arbitrary power and the violation of civil liberties, seem no longer to figure so prominently in public concern." David Garland, *The Culture of Control: Crime and Social Order in Contemporary Chicago* (Chicago: University of Chicago Press, 2001), 12.

34. What a person knowingly exposes to the public, even in his own home or office, is not a subject of Fourth Amendment protection. It is not protected under the Fourth Amendment unless there is a reasonable expectation of privacy. In this case, there is no reasonable expectation of privacy in a phone booth. *Katz v. United States*, 389 U.S. 347, 351–52 (1967).

35. Justice Harlan states that *Katz* has been interpreted too broadly. *Katz* was not meant to add anything to Fourth Amendment law, merely to restate the law developed in *Olmstead. United States v. White*, 401 U.S. 745, 780 (1971), dissent J. Harlan.

36. *Lawrence v. Texas*, 539 U.S. 558, 562 (2003).

37. A black male born in 1991 has a 29.4 percent chance of being imprisoned during his lifetime, while a white male born in the same year has a 4.4 percent chance of being imprisoned during his lifetime. Thomas P. Bonczar, *Prevalence of Imprisonment in the U.S. Population, 1974–2001*, U.S. Department of Justice, Bureau of Justice Statistics, August 2003, http://www.ojp.usdoj.gov/bjs/pub/pdf/piusp01.pdf.

38. The Violent Crime Control and Law Enforcement Act of 1994 eliminated Pell Grants for prisoners, abruptly ending the education of most and leaving only eight postsecondary programs in prisons across the country one year later. Joseph Fried, "Leaving Prison Doors Behind, Some Find New Doors Open," *New York Times*, October 18, 2006.

39. Glenn Loury, testimony, Senate Mass Incarceration Hearings, Washington, DC, October 4, 2007.

3. Justice on Drugs

1. Edward Huntington Williams, "Murder and Insanity Increasing Among Lower Class Because They Have Taken to 'Sniffing' Since Being Deprived of Whiskey by Prohibition," *New York Times*, February 8, 1914, Schaffer Library of Drug Policy, DRCNet Online Library of Drug Policy, http://www.druglibrary.org/SCHAFFER/History/negro_cocaine_fiends.htm.

2. Charles Whitebread, "The History of the Non-Medical Use of Drugs in the United States," Schaffer Library of Drug Policy, DRCNet Online Library of Drug Policy, http://www.druglibrary.org/schaffer/History/whiteb1.htm.

3. Omnibus Crime Control and Safe Streets Act (1968), 42 U.S.C. §3711.

4. U.S. Department of Justice, Bureau of Justice Statistics, "Persons Arrested," September 2007, http://www.fbi.gov/ucr/cius2006/arrests/index.html.

5. Christopher J. Mumola and Allen J. Beck, PhD, "Bureau of Justice Statistics Bulletin: Prisoners in 1996," U.S. Department of Justice, Office of Justice Programs, June 1997, http://www.ojp.usdoj.gov/bjs/pub/pdf/p01.pdf. The reason that so many people in the United States are locked up has little to do with violent crime. From 1975 until now, violent crime has actually decreased. The reason

that the incarceration rate has continued to rise is the War on Drugs. According to the U.S. Justice Department, between 1990 and 2000, "Overall, the percentage of violent Federal inmates declined from 17% to 10%. While the number of offenders in each major offense category increased, the number incarcerated for a drug offense accounted for the largest percentage of the total growth (59%), followed by public-order offenders (32%)." Paige M. Harrison and Allen J. Beck, PhD, "Bureau of Justice Statistics Bulletin: Prisoners in 2001," U.S. Department of Justice, Office of Justice Programs, July 2002, http://www.ojp.usdoj.gov/bjs/pub/pdf/ p01.pdf.

6. Adam Liptak, "American Exception: Inmate Count in U.S. Dwarfs Other Nations," *New York Times*, April 23, 2008, http://www.nytimes.com/2008/04/23/ us/23prison.html?_r=1&oref=slogin; see also William J. Sabol, PhD, Paige M. Harrison, and Heather Couture, "Bureau of Justice Statistics Bulletin: Prisoners in 2006," U.S. Department of Justice, Office of Justice Programs, December 2007, http://www.ojp.usdoj.gov/bjs/pub/pdf/p06.pdf.

7. Sabol, Harrison, and Couture, "Bureau of Justice Statistics Bulletin: Prisoners in 2006."

8. Ibid.; quote from Paul Justice, "What Every American Should Know About the Criminal Justice System," StopViolence.com, http://www.stopviolence.com/ cj-knowledge.htm.

9. Craig Haney, PhD, and Philip Zimbardo, PhD, "The Past and Future of U.S. Prison Policy: Twenty-Five Years After the Stanford Prison Experiment," *American Psychologist* 53, no. 7 (1998): 721.

10. U.S. Department of Justice, Bureau of Justice Statistics, *Sourcebook of Criminal Justice Statistics*, 1996, 476.

11. Douglas A. McVay, "Drug War Facts: Marijuana," Common Sense for Drug Policy, http://www.drugwarfacts.org/marijuana.htm. Information compiled from the FBI Uniform Crime Reports, 1990–2006. *Crime in America: FBI Uniform Crime Reports 2006* (Washington, DC: U.S. Department of Justice, 2007), Table 29, http://www.fbi.gov/ucr/cius2006/data/table_29.html; "Arrest Table: Arrests for Drug Abuse Violations," http://www.fbi.gov/ucr/cius2006/arrests/index .html (accessed September 24, 2007); *Crime in America: FBI Uniform Crime Reports 2005* (Washington, DC: U.S. Department of Justice, 2006), Table 29, http://www.fbi.gov/ucr/05cius/data/table_29.html; "Arrest Table: Arrests for Drug Abuse Violations," http://www.fbi.gov/ucr/05cius/arrests/index.html (accessed September 20, 2006); *Crime in America: FBI Uniform Crime Reports 2004* (Washington, DC: U.S. Government Printing Office, 2005), p. 278, Table 4.1, and p. 280 Table 29; *Crime in America: FBI Uniform Crime Reports 2003* (Washington, DC: U.S. Government Printing Office, 2004), 269, Table 4.1, and 270, Table 29; *Crime in America: FBI Uniform Crime Reports 2002* (Washington, DC: U.S. Government Printing Office, 2003), 234, Table 4.1, and 234, Table 29; *Crime in America: FBI Uniform Crime Reports 2001* (Washington, DC: U.S. Government Printing Office, 2002), 232, Table 4.1, and 233, Table 29; *Uniform Crime Reports for the United States 2000* (Washington, DC: U.S. Government Printing Office, 2001), 215–16, Tables 29 and 4.1; *Uniform Crime Reports for the United States 1999* (Washington, DC: U.S. Government Printing Office, 2000), 211–12; *Uni-

form Crime Reports for the United States 1998 (Washington, DC: U.S. Government Printing Office, 1999), 209–10; *Crime in America: FBI Uniform Crime Reports 1997* (Washington, DC: U.S. Government Printing Office, 1998), 221, Table 4.1, and 222, Table 29; *Crime in America: FBI Uniform Crime Reports 1996* (Washington, DC: U.S. Government Printing Office, 1997), 213, Table 4.1, and 214, Table 29; FBI Uniform Crime Reports for the United States 1995 (Washington, DC: U.S. Government Printing Office, 1996) 207–8; FBI Uniform Crime Reports for the United States 1990 (Washington, DC: U.S. Government Printing Office, 1991), 173–74.

12. Daniel Okrent, *Great Fortune: The Epic of Rockefeller Center* (New York: Viking Press, 2003).

13. Eric E. Sterling, "Drug Policy: A Challenge of Values," *Journal of Religion and Spirituality in Social Work* 24 (2004): 56. Obtained at Criminal Justice Policy Foundation, "Books and Resources," http://www.cjpf.org/booksandresources/challengeofvalues.pdf.

14. U.S. Department of Justice, Bureau of Justice Statistics, "Drug and Crime Facts," April 2007, http://www.ojp.usdoj.gov/bjs/dcf/du.htm#general.

15. National Institutes of Health, National Institute on Drug Abuse, "Monitoring the Future, 2007 Full Press Release on Drug Use from the University of Michigan," December 2007, http://www.nida.nih.gov/Newsroom/07/MTF2007Drug.pdf.

16. Sterling, "Drug Policy," 62.

17. This is because there is greater profit in the more potent form of the drug, and given the way the War on Drugs is structured, there is typically the same penalty for the strong form of the drug as the weaker form.

18. *United States v. Place*, 462 U.S. 696. Supreme Ct. of the U.S. June 20, 1983.

19. *Whren v. United States*, 517 U.S. 806. Supreme Ct. of the U.S. June 10, 1996.

20. *Schneckloth v. Bustamonte*, 412 U.S. 218. Supreme Ct. of the U.S. May 29, 1973.

21. *Vernonia School District 47J v. Wayne Action*, 515 U.S. 646. Supreme Ct. of the U.S. June 26, 1995.

22. *Hooper v. United States*, 547 U.S. 1199. Supreme Ct. of U.S. June 12, 2006.

23. Steven B. Duke, "Drug Prohibition: An Unnatural Disaster," *Connecticut Law Review* 27 (Winter 1995): 571.

24. Erik Grant Luna, "Our Vietnam: The Prohibition Apocalypse," *DePaul Law Review* 46 (Winter 1997): 483.

25. C.P. Rydell and S.S. Everingham, "Controlling Cocaine," Office of National Drug Control Policy, Drug Policy Research Center, RAND Corporation, 1994.

26. D.C. Des Jarlais, M. Marmor, D. Paone, et al., "HIV Incidence Among Injecting Drug Users in New York City Syringe Exchange Programs," *Americal Journal of Public Health* 90 (2000): 352–59. See also "Surgeon General's Needle Exchange Review," Update Requested by Representative Nancy Pelosi from the

Secretary of Health and Human Services, Donna Shalala, March 2000, http://www.csdp.org/research/surgeongennex.pdf.

27. Charlie Goodyear, "Pot Crimes May Get Less Police Attention: Supervisor Proposes Making Marijuana Busts a Low Priority," *San Francisco Chronicle*, September 12, 2006, http://www.sfgate.com/cgi-bin/article.cgi?f=/c/a/2006/09/12/BAGSPL3S1K1.DTL.

28. DanceSafe, June 27, 2007, http://www.dancesafe.org/documents/about/index.php.

29. "NIDA InfoFacts: Treatment Approaches for Drug Addiction," National Institute on Drug Abuse, National Institutes of Health, http://www.drugabuse.gov/infofacts/treatmeth.html.

30. Dana Graham, "Decriminalization of Marijuana: An Analysis of the Law in the United States and the Netherlands and Suggestions for Reform," *Loyola of Los Angeles International and Comparative Law Review* 23 (2001): 304.

31. On nicotine's addictive element: National Institutes of Health, National Institute on Drug Abuse, "NIDA InfoFacts: Cigarettes and Other Tobacco Products," July 2006, http://www.drugabuse.gov/Infofacts/Tobacco.html; see also Department of Health and Human Services, Centers for Disease Control and Prevention, "You Can Quit Smoking: Nicotine Addiction," February 2007, http://www.cdc.gov/tobacco/quit_smoking/you_can_quit/nicotine.htm. The National Institutes of Health estimates that alcohol and tobacco costs society about $320 billion annually. The costs of illegal drugs are $181 billion, but about $100 billion of that is for prison and court costs. "NIDA InfoFacts."

32. Department of Health and Human Services, Centers for Disease Control and Prevention, "Global Youth Tobacco Surveillance, 2000–2007," January 2008, http://www.cdc.gov/mmwr/preview/mmwrhtml/ss5701a1.htm.

4. Jury Duty: Power to the People

1. But see Chapter 6 for a discussion of the limits of my authority as a line prosecutor.

2. *United States v. Thomas*, 116 F.3d 606 2d Cir. (1997).

3. Indiana, Georgia, Maryland, and Oregon.

4. Within the constitutions of Indiana, Maryland, and Georgia, it is even stated that the jury shall be the judges of both law and facts. These similar provisions have been interpreted in differing ways, however. The Indiana supreme court held that it was reversible error for the trial judge not to instruct the jury that it had the right to determine the law for itself when the defendant requested such an instruction. See *Warren v. State*, 725 N.E.2d 828, 837 (Ind. 2000). The court of appeals of Maryland confines the jury's law-finding power to resolving conflicting interpretations of criminal statutes and deciding whether to apply law to questionable fact patterns. See *Stevenson v. State*, 423 A.2d 558, 564 (Md. 1980). The Oregon constitution states that the jury has the right to determine both law and fact, with the direction of the court as to the law. The Oregon supreme court has held this provision to simply be a statement of fact and that it does not allow a defen-

dant to ask for a nullification instruction. See *State v. Hoffman*, 677 P.2d 72, 73 (1984).

5. See, e.g., *Patterson v. Runnels*, 288 F. Supp. 2d 1092, 1100 (C.D. Cal. 2003); *United States v. Simpson*, 460 F.2d 515, 519 (9th Cir. 1972); *United States v. Moylan*, 417 F.2d 1002, 1006–07 (1969).

6. *People v. Kriho*, 996 P.2d 158 (Colo. App. 1999).

7. Bill Hutchinson, "Jurors Say Holes in Evidence, Not Race, Were Deciding Factors to Acquit Simpson," *Boston Herald*, October 5, 1995.

8. "Racially-Based Jury Nullification: Black Power in the Criminal Justice System," *Yale Law Journal* 105 (1995): 677.

9. "Jury Nullification and the Rule of Law," *Minnesota Law Review* 81 (1997): 1149.

5. Patriot Acts: Don't Be a Snitch, Do Be a Witness, and Don't Always Help the Police

1. These facts are taken from the following sources: Shaila Dewan and Brenda Goodman, "Prosecutors Say Corruption in Atlanta Police Dept Is Widespread," *New York Times*, April 27, 2007; Associated Press, "Family of Woman Killed by Police Sues," *New York Times*, November 22, 2007; Shaila Dewan and Brenda Goodman, "Anger Spills Over in Atlanta at Killing of Aged Woman," *New York Times*, November 29, 2006; Brenda Goodman, "Police Kill Woman, 92, in Shootout at Her Home," *New York Times*, November 23, 2006. Various news accounts portrayed Mrs. Johnston's age at either eighty-eight or ninety-two at the time of her death.

2. Dewan and Goodman, "Prosecutors Say Corruption in Atlanta Police Dept. Is Widespread."

3. American Civil Liberties Union, "Undercover, Unreliable and Unaddressed: Reconsidering the Use of Informants in Drug Law Enforcement," roundtable discussion transcript, Atlanta, GA, May 15, 2007, 8.

4. Ibid.

5. Greg Sandoval, "Shaq Won't Say If He'll Accept Kobe's Apology," *New York Times*, December 16, 2004.

6. "FBI FY 2008 Authorization and Budget Request to Congress," Federation of American Scientists, July 9, 2008, http://fas.org/irp/agency/doj/fbi/2008just.pdf, 4-22-4.25.

7. Office of the Inspector General, "Audit Report: The DEA's Payments to Confidential Sources," U.S. Department of Justice, July 2005, http://www.usdoj.gov/oig/reports/DEA/a05/index.htm.

8. "Sentences Within and Departing from U.S. Sentencing Commission Guidelines in U.S. District Court," *Sourcebook of Criminal Justice Statistics Online*, Table 5.34, http://www.albany.edu/sourcebook/pdf.t5362007.pdf.

9. "Offenders' Sentences in the U.S. District Court under the U.S. Sentencing Commission Guidelines," *Sourcebook of Criminal Justice Statistics Online*, Table 5.26, http://www.albany.edu/sourcebook/pdf.t5262007.

10. "Interview with Jim Boma," PBS, July 9, 2008, http://www.pbs.org/wgbh/pages/frontline/shows/snitch/cases/boma.html.

11. Jeremy Kahn, "The Story of a Snitch," *Atlantic*, April 2007, http://www.theatlantic.com/doc/200704/stop-snitching.

12. "Interview with Jim Boma."

13. See "Crime Pays Big for Informants in Forfeiture Drug Cases, Part Four: The Informants," *Pittsburgh Press*, February 27, 1991; Andrew E. Serwer, "The Hells Angels' Devilish Business," *Fortune*, November 30, 1992.

14. The Asset Forfeiture Fund's first priorities are to cover the costs of the program. After the costs are covered, it is determined if funds are available for investigative expenses, such as awards for information. Office of the Inspector General, "Seized Asset Forfeiture Fund Annual Financial Statement, Fiscal Year 2006," January 2007, U.S. Department of Justice, http://www.usdoj.gov/jmd/afp/01programaudit/fy2006/fy06_afs_report.pdf. State and local law enforcement receive "equitable sharing" for forfeiture they help to bring in under federal law. The equitable sharing program has distributed over $2 billion since 1986. Kayla Dunn, "Reining in Forfeiture: Common Sense Reform in the War on Drugs," *Frontline*, October 2000, http://www.pbs.org/wgbh/pages/frontline/shows/drugs/special/forfeiture.html (accessed July 9, 2008).

15. "Crime Pays Big for Informants in Forfeiture Drug Cases, Part Four: The Informants."

16. Ibid.

17. In the academy the strongest critiques of snitching have come from professors Alexandra Natapoff and Marc Lamont Hill. See Alexandra Natapoff, "Snitching: The Institutional and Communal Consequences," *University of Cincinnati Law Review* 73 (2004): 645; Alexandra Natapoff, "Beyond Unreliability: How Snitches Contribute to Wrongful Convictions," *Golden Gate University Law Review* 37 (2006): 107; Marc Lamont Hill, "The Barbershop Notebooks: Damned If You Do. Damned If You Don't," *Pop Matters*, February 24, 2006, http://www.popmatters.com/columns/hill/060224-1.shtml. See also Richard Rosenfield, "Snitching and the Code of the Street," *British Journal of Criminology* 43 (2003): 291. For a limited defense of snitching, see Dan Kahan and Tracey Meares, "Law and (Norms of) Order in the Inner City," *Law and Society Review* 32 (1998): 805–20.

18. "Eye to Eye: Cam'ron," *60 Minutes*, CBS, WUSA, Washington, April 22, 2007.

19. Kahn, "The Story of a Snitch."

20. Gary Gately, "Police Counter Dealers' DVD with One of Their Own," *New York Times*, May 11, 2005.

21. Only a few officers had ever made a complaint against another officer. One-third of the officers studied had been disciplined for some type of dishonesty (failing to report incidents they had witnessed, lying about their own involvement, or trying to cover for another officer). The commission referred to this disconnect between policy and practice as the "code of silence." Report of the Independent Commission on the Los Angeles Police Department, 1991, 132–33.

22. Gabriel J. Chin and Scott C. Wallace, "The Blue Wall of Silence as Evi-

dence of Bias and Motive to Lie: A New Approach to Police Perjury," *University of Pittsburgh Law Review* 59 (1998): 233, 237.

23. *Domenech v. City of New York*, 919 F. Supp. 702, 711 (S.D.N.Y. 1996).

24. Louise Westmarland, "Police Ethics and Integrity: Breaking the Blue Code of Silence," *Policing and Society* 15, no. 2 (2005): 145–65.

25. Rick Porrello, *The Rise and Fall of the Cleveland Mafia: Corn, Sugar, and Blood* (New York: Barricade Books, 1995), 23.

26. These sentiments are from Salvatore Gravano's testimony at the trial of John Gotti, which is quoted in the opinion. *United States v. Gotti*, 171 F.R.D. 19, 52 (E.D.N.Y. 1997).

27. To date, thirty-three states and the District of Columbia have recognized a journalists' privilege through enactment of press "shield laws." Another sixteen states have adopted a journalist's privilege through court decisions. Wyoming is the only state that does not have a journalist privilege through either statutory or case law. Henry Cohen, "Journalists' Privilege to Withhold Information in Judicial and Other Proceedings: State Shield Statutes," Congressional Research Service, June 27, 2007, 1.

28. "Judith Miller Goes to Jail," editorial, *New York Times*, July 7, 2005.

29. Out of a study of 111 cases of death-row wrongful convictions, 50 of the cases (45 percent) were caused by snitches. Rob Warden, "The Snitch System: How Snitch Testimony Sent Randy Steidl and Other Innocent Americans to Death Row," Center on Wrongful Convictions, Northwestern University Law School, 2004, 14.

30. Confidential informants may be authorized to conduct otherwise illegal activity as long the activity is necessary to either "obtain information of evidence essential for the success of an investigation that is not reasonably available without such authorization" or "to prevent death, serious bodily injury, or significant damage to property." The only restriction is that the benefits of the illegal activity (for the investigation) must outweigh the risks (to society). "The Attorney General's Guidelines Regarding the Use of Confidential Informants," U.S. Department of Justice, January 8, 2001, http://www.usdoj.gov/ag/readingroom/ciguidelines.htm.

31. Al Baker and Alan Feuer, "Officers' Arrests Put Spotlight on Police Use of Informants," *New York Times*, January 27, 2008.

32. Office of the Inspector General, "The Federal Bureau of Investigation's Compliance with the Attorney General's Investigative Guidelines," U.S. Department of Justice, September 2005, http://www.usdoj.gov/oig/special/0509/index.htm.

33. American Civil Liberties Union, "Undercover, Unreliable and Unaddressed," 11.

34. Associated Press, "Operation TIPS Trips Up?" CBS, August 8, 2002, http://www.cbsnews.com/stories/2002/08/10/national/main518273.shtml.

35. Julia Scheeres, "Feds' Spying Plan Fades to Black," *Wired*, December 4, 2002.

36. In pertinent part, the statute states that "whoever, having knowledge of the actual commission of a felony cognizable by a court of the United States, conceals

and does not as soon as possible make known the same to some judge or other person in civil or military authority under the United States, shall be fined under this title or imprisoned not more than three years, or both." 18 U.S.C. 4 (2008).

37. Michael Fortier served a prison sentence for his role in carrying out the bombing (transporting weapons). His wife was also aware of the bombing beforehand, but was not prosecuted. Ralph Blumenthal, "Release of Oklahoma City Bombing Figure Kindles Fears," *New York Times*, January 19, 2006.

38. Sanford Kadish and Stephen Schulhofer, *Criminal Law and Its Processes*, 6th ed. (New York: Aspen Publishers, 1995), 186.

39. Jon Kleining, "Good Samaritanism," *Philosophy and Public Affairs* 5 (1976): 382.

40. Law enforcement agencies clear a case when an offender is arrested or if there are exceptional circumstances. Exceptional circumstances include identification of the offender, gathering enough evidence to support an arrest and make a charge, and encountering circumstances outside the control of law enforcement (including, but not limited to: suicide of the offender, refusal of victim to cooperate, and denial of extradition). In 2006, law enforcement cleared 44.3 percent of violent crimes and 15.8 percent of property crimes. Federal Bureau of Investigation, "Clearances," *Crime in the United States 2006*, http://www.fbi.gov/ucr/cius 2006/offenses/clearances/index.html.

41. Touré, "A Snitch Like Me," *New York Times*, March 23, 2008.

42. The Supreme Court has created many exceptions to this general rule, including for frisks of crime suspects, *Terry v. Ohio*, 392 U.S. 1, 13 (1968); drug testing of some public school students, *Vernonia School District v. Acton*, 515 U.S. 646, 653 (1995); *Chandler v. Miller*, 520 U.S. 305, 313 (1997); and searches of people entering or leaving the United States, *United States v. Ramsey*, 431 U.S. 606, 616 (1977).

6. Should Good People Be Prosecutors?

1. Abbe Smith, "Can You Be a Good Person and a Good Prosecutor?" *Georgetown Journal of Legal Ethics* 14 (2001): 355.

2. Ibid., 396.

3. Ellis Cose, ed. "The Darden Dilemma," *Black Writers on Justice, Race, and Conflicting Loyalties* (New York: HarperCollins, 2003), 12; Kenneth B. Nunn, "The 'Darden Dilemma': Should African Americans Prosecute Crimes?" *Fordham Law Review* 68 (2000): 1473; Lenese C. Herbert, "Loyalty and Criminal Justice: A Mini-Symposium: Et in Arcadia Ego: A Perspective on Black Prosecutors' Loyalty Within the American Criminal Justice System," *Howard Law Journal* 49 (2006): 495; Margaret M. Russel, "Symposium: Representing Race: Beyond 'Sellouts' and 'Race Cards': Black Attorneys and the Straightjacket of Legal Practice," *Michigan Law Review* 95 (1997): 766; David B. Wilkins, "Symposium: Representing Race: Straightjacketing Professionalism: A Comment on Russel," *Michigan Law Review* 95 (1997): 795; Felicia J. Nu'Man, "I Am Not the Enemy; I Put People in Jail Because They Break the Law, Not Because I'm a Puppet of a Racist Judicial System," *Newsweek*, April 14, 2008.

4. These cases have primarily concerned jurors. *Georgia v. McCollum*, 505 U.S. 42 (1992); *Batson v. Kentucky*, 476 U.S. 79 (1986).

5. Eric Lotke, *Hobbling a Generation: Young African American Males in Washington D.C.'s Criminal Justice System Five Years Later*, National Center on Institutions and Alternatives, 1997.

6. Angela J. Davis, *Arbitrary Justice: The Power of the American Prosecutor* (New York: Oxford University Press, 2007).

7. In *United States v. Booker*, the court held that the federal sentencing guidelines are advisory rather than binding on judges. *United States v. Booker*, 543 U.S. 220 (2005).

8. U.S.C., Crimes, Firearms, sec. 924(c)(1)(A). See also *United States v. Watson*, No. 06-571 2007.

9. In some jurisdictions the executive can fire the head prosecutor. A salient example is the "Saturday Night Massacre," in which former president Nixon triggered a series of resignations while forcing the firing of a prosecutor. See Neil A. Lewis, "Elliot Richardson Dies at 79; Stood Up to Nixon and Resigned in 'Saturday Night Massacre,' " *New York Times*, January 1, 2000.

10. Amy Goldstein, "Fired Prosecutor Says Gonzales Pushed the Death Penalty, Figures Show Attorney General Often Overrules US Attorneys' Arguments Against Capital Charges," *Washington Post*, June 28, 2007, A07.

11. William J. Stuntz, "The Pathological Politics of Criminal Law," *Michigan Law Review* 100 (2001): 505.

12. Tracey L. Meares, "Social Organization and Drug Law Enforcement," *American Criminal Law Review* 35 (1998): 191.

13. Dan M. Kahan, "A Colloquium on Community Policing: Reciprocity, Collective Action and Community Policing," *California Law Review* 90 (2002): 1513; Randall Kennedy, *Race, Crime, and the Law* (New York: Pantheon Books, 1997).

14. David Barstow and Duff Wilson, "Charges of Rape Against 3 at Duke Are Dropped," *New York Times*, December 23, 2006, http://www.nytimes.com/2006/12/23/sports/23duke.html.

15. Daryl Fears, "L.A. Town Fells 'White Tree,' but Tension Runs Deep," *Washington Post*, August 4, 2007, A03; Mary Foster, "Judges Differ over Opening 'Jena 6' Records: One Plans Appeal to Keep Court Proceedings Closed in Teen's Beating Case," *Washington Post*, December 9, 2007, A04.

16. Dan Eggen and Michael A. Fletcher, "Embattled Gonzales Resigns: Attorney General Was Criticized for Terrorism Policy, Prosecutor Firings," *Washington Post*, August 28, 2007, A01.

17. Adam Liptak, "Prosecutor Becomes Prosecuted," *New York Times*, June 24, 2007, http://query.nytimes.com/gst/fullpage.html?res=9900E1DC1E3FF937A15755C0A9619C8B63.

18. Vivian S. Toy, "Prosecutor Is Berated by Giuliani," *New York Times*, May 25, 1996, http://query.nytimes.com/gst/fullpage.html?res=9C00E4D6163BF935A3575AC0A960958260; Jan Hoffman, "Factions on Death Penalty Issue Gird for Battle," *New York Times*, September 6, 1996, http://query.nytimes.com/gst/fullpage.html?res=9C00E4D6163BF935A3575AC0A960958260.

19. Bill Hopkins, "DA Hallinan the Survivor," *San Francisco Frontlines*, November 24, 2003.

20. Duncan Kennedy, "Rebels from Principle: Changing the Corporate Law Firm from Within," *Harvard Law School Bulletin*, Fall 1981, 39.

21. It should go without saying that I wish racial disparities did not exist. A 3–1 black-white disparity is not close to ideal, in the same way that 1,500,000 people in prison is still too many. To the extent that most black-white racial disparities reflect socioeconomic deprivations suffered by African Americans, we would expect to see those deprivations reflected in criminal justice. My "goal" here—to bring disparities in criminal justice closer to the level of other racial disparities—is modest, because I intend for it to be achievable in the short term. My ultimate aspiration is for no racial disparities at all in criminal justice, but we shall not see that day until African Americans have equal access to education, health care, and capital. Those goals are not, unfortunately, likely to be achieved anytime soon.

7. A Hip-Hop Theory of Justice

1. Nas, "If I Ruled the World," *It Was Written* (Sony Records, 1996), lyrics available at Original Hip-Hop (Rap) Lyrics Archive, http://www.ohhla.com/anonymous/nas/written/ruled.nas.txt (accessed March 28, 2004).

2. The hip-hop nation consists of artists, students, workers, activists, and scholars. For a discussion of the distinction between the hip-hop generation and Generation X, see Gary Mendez, "Confessions of a Gen Xpatriate: Pledging Allegiance to the Hip-Hop Generation," http://www.horizonmag.com/3/gen-xpatriate.asp (accessed March 28, 2004).

3. Jay-Z, "Justify My Thug," *The Black Album* (Roc-A-Fella Records, 2003), lyrics available at Original Hip-Hop (Rap) Lyrics Archive, http://www.ohhla.com/anonymous/jigga/theblack/justify.jyz.txt (accessed March 4, 2004).

4. Beanie Sigel, "What Your Life Like," *The Truth* (Def Jam Records, 2000), lyrics available at Original Hip-Hop (Rap) Lyrics Archive, http://www.ohhla.com/anonymous/beanie/thetruth/whatlife.sig.txt (accessed March 7, 2004).

5. The phrase comes from Chuck D, of the rap group Public Enemy. See "The History of Hip-Hop," http://www.headbob.com/hiphop/hiphophistory.shtml (accessed March 28, 2004).

6. See Matt Benz, "Rock Still the Top-Selling Genre," *Billboard*, March 31, 2001, 6, 86 (explaining that hip-hop overtook country music as the second most popular genre of music); Todd Martens, "Rock Tops RIAA Poll," *Billboard*, May 31, 2003, 74 (reporting that the market share of rap/hip-hop grew from 11.4 percent to 13.8 percent, second only to rock). In 2003, for the first time, the top ten songs on the Billboard Hot 100 were all by African American artists. Gail Mitchell, "Black-Music's Historic Week: Hot 100 Testifies to Mainstreaming of R&B/Hip-Hop," *Billboard*, October 18, 2003, 20.

7. See Alan Hughes, "Hip-Hop Economy," *Black Enterprise*, May 2002 (describing the money generated by various hip-hop businesses), available at http://www.blackenterprise.com/Pageopen.asp?Source-Articles/01012002ah.html (accessed March 28, 2004).

8. See U.S. Census Bureau, "Projections of the Resident Population by Race, Hispanic Origin and Nativity: Middle Series, 2050 to 2070" (reporting that in 2050 almost 50 percent of Americans will be either African American, Hispanic, Asian American, or Native American), available at http://www.census.gov/popula tion/projections/nation/summary/np-t5-g.text (accessed March 28, 2004).

9. See Lynette Holloway, "The Angry Appeal of Eminem Is Cutting Across Racial Lines," *New York Times*, October 28, 2002, C1 (noting how "three decades [after the creation of hip-hop], the No. 1 selling rapper in the country is a 30-year-old white man, Eminem"); Brad Tyler, "Houston: A Hot Spot for Hip-Hop; the Scene on Rap's Third-Coast Benefits from Local and Latino Support," *Billboard*, September 23, 2000, 32 (describing the influence of Latino Rap in Houston). Asian hip-hop artists have also made inroads. Chinese-American rapper Jin won BET's recent rap contest. His debut album is highly anticipated. See Raymond Fiore, "Jin's Bad Rap: Is This Asian-American MC's Debut Making History or Rehashing Old Stereotypes?" *Entertainment Weekly*, February 13, 2004, L2T3. Best-selling singer Sean Paul, known for blending Jamaican dance hall music with hip-hop, is half Chinese. Shelah Moody, "Jamaica Meets Hip-Hop: Dance Hall Fuses Styles and Finds an Audience," *San Francisco Chronicle*, March 23, 2003, 27 (explaining that "Sean Paul has a unique, racially ambiguous look [he is black, Portuguese and Chinese] that various ethnic groups can identify with").

10. See Lynette Holloway, "The Angry Appeal of Eminem Is Cutting Across Racial Lines," *New York Times*, October 28, 2002 (noting that "it is well known among music industry executives that hip-hop consumers are more than 75 percent nonblack").

11. See Marc Mauer, *Race to Incarcerate* (New York: The New Press, 1999), 125 (reporting that the lifetime likelihood of imprisonment for a male born in 1991 would be 29 percent if he were African American, 16 percent if he were Latino, and only 4 percent if he were white; citing Thomas P. Bonczar and Allen J. Beck, "Lifetime Likelihood of Going to State or Federal Prison," Bureau of Justice Statistics 1997).

12. See Federal Election Commission, "Voter Registration and Turnout by Age, Gender and Race 1998," 1998 (reporting that those between the ages of 18–24 made up only 5.1% of the total vote in the 1998 general elections), available at http://www.fec.gov/pages/98demog.htm (accessed March 5, 2004).

13. See Peter Baker, "Clinton Would Cut Disparity in Some Cocaine Sentences," *Washington Post*, July 23, 1997, A21.

14. This account is taken from "The History of Hip-Hop."

15. Ibid.

16. Ibid.

17. Ibid.

18. Ibid.

19. See *Wild Style* (Rhino, 1982) for a fictionalized film version of the dawn of hip-hop culture.

20. See Baruit N. Kopano, "Rap Music as an Extension of the Black Rhetorical Tradition: 'Keepin It Real,'" *Western Journal of Black Studies* 26 (Winter 2002): 204 (describing the rich gradations of rap music and explaining that "it is a

legacy that may go as far back as the griots of West Africa"); "Keeping Up with Jones: Quincy Jones, Pop Legend," *Interview*, November 1995, 28 (quoting Quincy Jones as noting that "rappers may not realize how deep the roots are with the griots from West Africa").

21. Ibid.

22. Ibid.

23. Ibid.

24. See Jon Pareles, "Outlaw Rock: More Skirmishes on the Censorship Front," *New York Times*, December 10, 1989, 2, 32; Juan Williams, "Fighting Words; Speaking Out Against Racism, Sexism and Gay-Bashing in Pop," *Washington Post*, October 15, 1989, G1.

25. Teresa Wiltz, "We the Peeps: After Three Decades Chillin' in the Hood, Hip-Hop Is Finding Its Voice Politically," *Washington Post*, June 25, 2002, C1.

26. Ibid. The author Bakari Kitwana has also described "two sides" to hip-hop. He states:

> Hip-hop has a positive impact, but also has a negative impact in terms of these anti-black images and this misogynistic attitude that comes from rappers who sell multi-platinum records. Like Jay-Z. But at the same time Jay-Z offers a message that the society is screwed up, that it's difficult out here, that the issues of unemployment and education are critical issues. The music is contradictory but the messages that society is sending us are contradictory too. I don't think that it's unusual; I think that's how life is.

See also Suzy Hansen, "Hip-Hop Nation," *Salon*, July 19, 2002 (quoting Bakari Kitwana), available at http://archive.salon.com/books/int/2002/07/10/kitwana/ (accessed March 31, 2004). Many hip-hop artists cannot be placed in either category. Eminem, for example, is the best-selling rap artist in history, and his music is neither political nor gangsta.

27. See Mary Ellen Walker, "The Kids' Reading Room: Top of the News," *Los Angeles Times*, February 26, 1999, E8 (noting Hill's was the first hip-hop album to win the Grammy for album of the year).

28. See Geoff Boucher, "The Grammy Awards," *Los Angeles Times*, February 28, 2002, pt. 1, 13 (noting that, in 2002, Alicia Keys won five Grammy awards, including best new artist and song of the year); "46th Annual Grammys: Complete List of Winners," *Billboard*, February 21, 2004, 70 (noting OutKast's *Speakerboxxx/The Love Below* won the Grammy for album of the year).

29. See Cornel West, "Nihilism in the Black Community," *Dissent* (1991): 221.

30. See Kelefa Sanneh, "Music: The Highs; the Albums and Songs of the Year," *New York Times*, December 28, 2003, 2, 31 (noting how 50 Cent's "casual jokes about death are his way of reminding us of the price he might have to pay for his success—and for our entertainment").

31. See Holloway, "Angry Appeal of Eminem."

32. See Jeffrey McKinney, "From Rags to Riches: Hip-Hop Moguls Use Groundbreaking Designs and Star Power to Challenge Major Clothing Labels

and Become a Force in the $164 Billion Fashion Industry," *Black Enterprise*, September 2002, available at http://www.blackenterprise.com/printarticle.asp?source-/archive2002/09/0902-41.htm (accessed January 31, 2004).

33. See John L. Mitchell, "Baggin' and Saggin': Parents Wary of a Big Fashion Trend," *Los Angeles Times*, September 28, 1992, B1 (reporting that the "trend toward baggy clothing was started by some of Los Angeles' toughest gangs, emulating the garb of prison inmates whose pants perpetually sag because prisoners are not issued belts"); Guy Trebay, "Maturing Rappers Try a New Uniform: Yo, a Suit!" *New York Times*, February 6, 2004, A1 (explaining "for most of the past decade, hip-hop credibility was linked to looking 'street,' a notion interpreted through styles that made reference to gang life [colored bandannas], the jailhouse [beltless jeans worn with one leg rolled] and subcultures in which the markers of cool were enmeshed in drug running and other activities as illicit as they were perversely glamorous").

34. See Dasun Allah, "The Swami of Hip-Hop: Russell Simmons Morphs into a Mogul-Activist," *Village Voice*, September 4, 2002, available at http://village voice.com/issues/0236/allah.php (accessed January 31, 2004).

35. Hip-Hop Summit Action Network, "Our Mission," http://www.hip hopsummitactionnetwork.org/content/main.aspx?pageid=7 (accessed March 5, 2004).

36. Hip-Hop Summit Action Network, "What We Want," http://www.hip hopsummitactionnetwork.org/Content/main.aspx?pageid=27 (accessed March 28, 2004).

37. Hip-Hop Summit Action Network, "Growing National Momentum Builds for 'Countdown to Fairness' Campaign to Repeal Rockefeller Drug Laws in New York," press release, May 12, 2003, available at http://www.hiphopsum mitactionnetwork.org/media/PDF/oldPressReleases/GROWING.pdf (accessed March 28, 2004).

38. Hip-Hop Summit Action Network, "Russell Simmons, Sean 'P. Diddy' Combs and the Hip-Hop Summit Action Network Together with Andrew Cuomo and the Mothers of the NY Disappeared to Announce Final 7-Day Countdown to Massive Rally at City Hall/Foley Square," media advisory, May 27, 2003, available at http://www.hiphopsummitactionnetwork.org/media/PDF/oldPressReleases/May28thAdvisoy.pdf (accessed March 28, 2004).

39. Hip-Hop Summit Action Network, "Growing National Momentum."

40. See Ta-Nehisi Coates, "Compa$$ionate Capitali$m: Russell $immons Wants to Fatten the Hip-Hop Vote—and Maybe His Wallet, Too," *Village Voice*, December 30, 2003.

41. National Hip-Hop Political Convention, http://www.hiphopconvention .org (accessed February 5, 2004).

42. See Davey D's Hip Hop Corner, http://www.daveyd.com (accessed March 5, 2004); the Hip-Hop Summit Action Network, http://www.hiphop sum mitactionnetwork.org (accessed March 5, 2004); the Temple of Hip Hop, http://www.templeofhiphop.org (accessed March 5, 2004).

43. Black Entertainment Television, "What's in It for Us? Barack Obama and the Black Vote," January 21, 2008.

44. See Federal Election Commission, "Voter Registration and Turnout by Age, Gender and Race, 1998."

45. See Alan Feuer, "Metro Briefing New York: Brooklyn: Combs Trial Figure Arrested," *New York Times*, June 15, 2001, B6 (reporting that P. Diddy was arrested for violating a federal weapons law); Robert D. McFadden, "Corrections Officer and Visiting Policeman Shot After Assault at Midtown Club," *New York Times*, March 6, 2000, B3 (reporting that Jay-Z was arrested for stabbing record promoter Lance Rivera at a night club); Lola Ogunnaike, "Amid Much Anticipation, a Rap Artist Makes a Debut," *New York Times*, February 6, 2003, E1 (reporting that former crack dealer 50 Cent was arrested for possession of two loaded handguns).

46. "Operation Lockdown," *Source*, March 2004, 107.

47. Ibid. The artists included Shyne, Chi-Ali, and Mystikal.

48. See Pierre Thomas, "1 in 3 Young Black Men in Justice System," *Washington Post*, October 5, 1995, A1; see also Mauer, *Race to Incarcerate*, 125 (citing Bonczar and Beck, "Bureau of Justice Statistics Special Report: Lifetime Likelihood of Going to State or Federal Prison," describing an earlier study in which the statistics was one in four).

49. Mauer, *Race to Incarcerate*, 125.

50. See Fox Butterfield, "Study Finds Big Increase in Black Men as Inmates Since 1980," *New York Times*, August 28, 2002, A14 (discussing a study that found that there are more black men in prison than in colleges or universities).

51. Big L featuring Fat Joe, "The Enemy," *The Big Picture* (Priority Records, 2000), lyrics available at Original Hip-Hop (Rap) Lyrics Archive, http://www.ohhla.com/anonymous/ditc/ditc/da_enemy.dtc.txt (accessed March 7, 2004).

52. See Michel Foucault, *Discipline and Punish: The Birth of the Prison*, trans. Alan Sheridan (New York: Vintage Books, 1977), 277–78.

53. Jay-Z, "A Ballad for the Fallen Soldier."

54. American films like *The Godfather* (Paramount, 1972), *Scarface* (Universal Studios, 1983), *Pulp Fiction* (Miramax Home Entertainment, 1994), and *American Gangster* (Universal Pictures, 2007), like gangsta rap, depict criminals as imperfect heroes.

55. See G-Unit, "G'up," *Beg for Mercy* (Interscope, 2003), lyrics available at Original Hip-Hop (Rap) Lyrics Archive, http://www.ohhla.com/anonymous/g_unit/begmercy/gd_up.unt.txt (accessed March 12, 2004) ("Cocaine, heroin, ecstasy, marijuana / I'm mule on that Greyhound from NY to the Carolina / Paper chase, different name, same face, don't catch a case"); Jay-Z featuring Babyface and Foxy Brown, "Sunshine," *In My Lifetime, Volume 1* (Universal, 1997), lyrics available at Original Hip-Hop (Rap) Lyrics Archive, http://www.ohhla.com/anonymous/jigga/lifetime/sunshine.jyz.txt (accessed March 12, 2004) ("If I needed would you give me your kidneys? [Uhh, uhh, fo'sho'] / Catch a case you catch it with me? [Mmm, fo'sho']").

56. See Tracey L. Meares, "Social Organization and Drug Law Enforcement," *American Criminal Law Review* 35 (1998): 191.

57. Robin D.G. Kelley, "Kickin' Reality, Kickin' Ballistics: Gangsta Rap and Postindustrial Los Angeles," in *Droppin' Science: Critical Essays on Rap Music*

and Hip-Hop Culture, ed. William Eric Perkins (Philadelphia: Temple University Press, 1996), 135.

58. Hieroglyphics, "All Things," *Third Eye Vision* (Hieroglyphics Imperium Records, 1998), lyrics available at Original Hip-Hop (Rap) Lyrics Archive, http://www.ohhla.com/anonymous/hiero/thirdeye/things.hie.txt (accessed March 5, 2004).

59. Michel Foucault, "Intellectuals and Power," in *Language, Counter-Memory, Practice: Selected Essays and Interviews*, ed. Donald F. Bouchard, trans. Donald F. Bouchard and Sherry Simon (Ithaca, NY: Cornell University Press, 1977), 205, 209.

60. See John Rawls, *A Theory of Justice* (Cambridge, MA: Belknap Press of Harvard University Press, 1971), advancing this theory.

61. For hip-hop songs expressing sympathy for victims of crime, see Ice Cube, "Dead Homiez," *Kill at Will* (Priority Records, 1990), lyrics available at Original Hip-Hop (Rap) Lyrics Archive, http://www.ohhla.com/anonymous/ice_cube/kill-will/homiez.cub.t xt (accessed March 4, 2004); Stop the Violence All-Stars, "Self Destruction," *Self Destruction 12?* (1989), lyrics available at Original Hip-Hop (Rap) Lyrics Archive, http://www.ohhla.com/anonymous/misc/hip-hop/self_des .stv.txt (accessed March 4, 2004); the West Coast Rap All-Stars, "We're All in the Same Gang," *We're All in the Same Gang* (Warner Brothers Records, 1990), lyrics available at Original Hip-Hop (Rap) Lyrics Archive, http://www.ohhla.com/anonymous/rap_comp/samegang/samegang.gng.txt (accessed March 4, 2004).

62. See U.S. Department of Justice, "Criminal Victimization in the United States, 2000 Statistical Tables," table 6, 2002, (finding victimization rates for all personal crimes for males age twelve and over to be 45.1 percent for black men compared to 32.8 percent for white men) available at http://www.ojp.gov/bjs/pub/pdg/cvus00.pdf (accessed March 1, 2004), ibid., table 8 (finding victimization rates for crimes of violence for Hispanic males age twelve and over to be 33.2 percent compared to 32.7 percent for non-Hispanic males age twelve and over).

63. For a discussion of the "broken window" theory of law enforcement, see James Q. Wilson and George L. Kelling, "Broken Windows," *Atlantic Monthly*, March 1982, 29. For a reaction from hip-hop to former New York City mayor Rudolph Giuliani's endorsement of "zero tolerance" policing, see Brand Nubian, "Probable Cause," *Foundation* (Arista Records, 1998), lyrics available at Original Hip-Hop (Rap) Lyrics Archive, http://ohhla.com/anonymous/brnubian/found/probable.brn.txt (accessed March 7, 2004) ("I ain't do shit! Jakes lock a nigga with a weed clip . . . Now Giuliani wanna talk about the 'Quality of Life' / Think he got the right to follow me at night / with no probable cause, other than my skin is black like yours").

64. Eve, "Love Is Blind," *Ruff Ryders' First Lady* (Interscope Records, 1999), lyrics available at Original Hip-Hop (Rap) Lyrics Archive, http://www.ohhla.com/anonymous/eve/firstldy/is_blind.eve.txt (accessed March 5, 2004).

65. Eve, "Love Is Blind."

66. Nelly, "Nellyville," *Nellyville* (Universal Records, 2002), lyrics available at Original Hip-Hop (Rap) Lyrics Archive, http://www.ohhla.com/anonymous/nelly/ville/nv.nel.txt (accessed March 5, 2004). For other examples of retribu-

tivism, see Notorious B.I.G., "Somebody's Gotta Die," *Life After Death* (Bad Boy Records, 1997); Mystikal, "Murder 2," *Unpredictable* (Jive Records, 1997).

67. Angie Stone, "Brotha," *Mahogany Soul* (J-Records, 2001), lyrics available at Lyrics Time, "Angie Stone Lyrics—Brotha (Remix)," http://www.lyricstime .com/lyrics/2682.html (accessed February 4, 2004).

68. Lost Boyz, "Jeeps, Lex Coups, Bimaz and Benz," *Legal Drug Money* (Uptown Records, 1996), lyrics available at Lyrics Search @ Astraweb, http://lyrics .astraweb.com/display/991/lost_boyz..legal_drug_money..jeeps_lex_coups_bimaz _and_benz.html.

69. A definition for the term "dis" can be found at urbandictionary.com, http://www.urbandictionary.com/define.php?term=dis&f=1 (accessed March 5, 2004).

70. A definition of the term "props" can be found at urbandictionary.com, http://www.urbandictionary.com/define.php?term=props&f=1 (accessed March 5, 2004).

71. See Michelle Goodwin, "The Economy of Citizenship," *Temple Law Review* 76 (2003), 129, 192, (discussing misogyny in rap music and noting how "Ice T, Ice Cube, Dr. Dre, Snoop Dogg, NWA, Slick Rick . . . and many more contribute to the denigration of women").

72. The philosopher Immanuel Kant's famous exposition of retribution is "Even if a Civil Society resolved to dissolve itself . . . the last Murderer lying in the prison ought to be executed before the resolution was carried out. . . . This ought to be done in order that every one may realize the desert of his deeds." See Sanford H. Kadish and Stephen J. Schulhofer, *Criminal Law and Its Processes: Cases and Materials*, 6th ed. (Boston: Little, Brown, 1995), 102–3.

73. See *Lockyer v. Andrade*, 538 U.S. 63 (2003) (upholding the constitutionality of a defendant's sentence to two consecutive terms of twenty-five years to life for stealing $68.84 worth of videotapes from a K-Mart store); *Harmelin v. Michigan*, 501 U.S. 957 (1991) (upholding a defendant's sentence of life without parole for possession of cocaine).

74. "Retributivism is based on the view that humans generally possess free will (or, perhaps more usefully, the capacity for free choice), and, therefore, may justly be blamed when they choose to violate society's mores." From Joshua Dressler, *Understanding Criminal Law*, 3d ed. (New York: Matthew Bender, 2001), 16.

75. See Kelley, "Kickin' Reality" ("Moreover, economic restructuring resulting in massive unemployment has created criminals out of black youth, which is what gangsta rappers acknowledge. But rather than apologize or preach, they attempt to rationalize and explain").

76. Jay-Z, "Dope Man," *Volume 3: The Life and Times of S. Carter* (Roc-A-Fella Records, 1999), lyrics available at Original Hip-Hop (Rap) Lyrics Archive, http://www.ohhla.com/anonymous/jigga/volume_3/dope_man.jyz.txt (accessed March 5, 2000). For a similar perspective, see Ice Cube, *Kill at Will* (Priority Records, 1990).

77. OutKast, "Mainstream," *ATLiens* (LaFace Records, 1996), lyrics available at Original Hip-Hop (Rap) Lyrics Archive, http://www.ohhla.com/anonymous/ outkast/atliens/main.otk.txt (accessed March 5, 2004).

78. NWA, "100 Miles and Runnin'," *100 Miles and Runnin'* (Priority Records, 1990), lyrics available at Original Hip-Hop (Rap) Lyrics Archive, http://www .ohhla.com/anonymous/nwa/100_mile/100_mile.nwa.txt (accessed March 5, 2004).

79. Erykah Badu, "The Other Side of the Game," *Baduizm* (Universal Records, 1997), lyrics available at Original Hip-Hop (Rap) Lyrics Archive, http://www.ohhla.com/anonymous/badu/baduizm/other.bdu.txt (accessed March 5, 2004).

80. See Dorothy E. Roberts, "The Social and Moral Cost of Mass Incarceration in African American Communities," *Stanford Law Review* 56 (2004): 1271.

81. See Todd R. Clear, "The Problem with 'Addition by Subtraction': The Prison-Crime Relationship in Low-Income Communities," in *Invisible Punishment: The Collateral Consequences of Mass Imprisonment*, ed. Marc Mauer and Meda Chesney-Lind (New York: The New Press, 2002), 181, 184 (describing urban areas in which one in four men is incarcerated).

82. Makaveli, "White Man'z World," *The Don Killuminati: The 7 Day Theory* (Interscope Records, 1996), lyrics available at Original Hip-Hop (Rap) Lyrics Archive, http://www.ohhla.com/anonymous/2_pac/don_kill/whiteman.2pc.txt (accessed March 5, 2004).

83. See Darryl K. Brown, "Third-Party Interests in Criminal Law," *Texas Law Review* 80 (2002): 1383 (discussing ways in which "the practice of criminal law . . . accommodates concerns for collateral consequences to third parties").

84. Kant wrote:

> Juridical Punishment can never be administered merely as a means of promoting another Good either with regard to the Criminal himself or to Civil Society, but must in all cases be imposed only because the individual on whom it is inflicted has committed a Crime. For one man ought never to be dealt with merely as a means subservient to the purpose of another . . .

Kant, *The Philosophy of Law*, 195 (emphasis in original).

85. Brown, "Third-Party Interests" (quoting memorandum from Eric H. Holder Jr., assistant attorney general, to all U.S. attorneys and heads of department components, pt. II [June 16, 1999]).

86. See *R. v. Gladue*, [1999] S.C.R. 688 (Can.).

87. Immortal Technique, "Peruvian Cocaine," *Revolutionary Volume 2* (Nature Sounds Records, 2003), lyrics available at Original Hip-Hop (Rap) Lyrics Archive, http://www.ohhla.com/anonymous/immortal/rev_vol2/peruvian.tch.txt (accessed March 5, 2004). Immortal Technique quotes this line from the movie *New Jack City* (Warner Brothers, 1991).

88. See Mauer, *Race to Incarcerate*, 124.

89. Ice-T, "Straight Up Nigga," *O.G. Original Gangster* (Warner Brothers Records, 1991), lyrics available at Original Hip-Hop (Rap) Lyrics Archive, http:// www.ohhla.com/anonymous/ice_t/og/straight.ict.txt (accessed March 5, 2004).

90. Immortal Technique, "Speak Your Mind," *Revolutionary Volume 1* (Viper Records, 2001), lyrics available at Original Hip-Hop (Rap) Lyrics Archive,

http://www.ohhla.com/anonymous/immortal/rev_vol1/speak_yr.tch.txt (accessed March 5, 2004).

91. Talib Kweli featuring Cocoa Brovaz, "Gun Music," *Quality* (MCA Records, 2002), lyrics available at Original Hip-Hop (Rap) Lyrics Archive, http://www.ohhla.com/anonymous/t_kweli/quality/gunmusic.tab.txt (accessed March 5, 2004).

92. Talib Kweli, "The Proud," *Quality*, lyrics available at Original Hip-Hop (Rap) Lyrics Archive, http://www.ohhla.com/anonymous/t_kweli/quality/the proud.tab.txt (last visited March 5, 2004).

93. Boogie Down Productions, "Illegal Business," *By All Means Necessary* (Jive Records, 1988), lyrics available at Original Hip-Hop (Rap) Lyrics Archive, http://www.ohhla.com/anonymous/boogiedp/by_all/business.bdp.txt (last visited March 4, 2004).

94. Erykah Badu, "Danger," *Worldwide Underground* (Motown Records, 2003), lyrics available at A-Z Lyrics Universe, http://www.azlyrics.com/lyrics/erykahbadu/danger.html (accessed March 5, 2004).

95. See Mauer, *Race to Incarcerate*, 147.

96. See Thomas, "1 in 3 Young Black Men."

97. For an insightful analysis of hip-hop's treatment of marijuana and crack cocaine, see Ted Sampsell-Jones, "Culture and Contempt: The Limitations of Expressive Criminal Law," *Seattle University Law Review* 27 (2003): 133, 163–67.

98. Ja Rule featuring Missy Elliot and Tweet, "X," *Pain Is Love* (Sony Records, 2001), lyrics available at Original Hip-Hop (Rap) Lyrics Archive, http://www.ohhla.com/anonymous/ja_rule/painlove/x.jah.txt (accessed March 7, 2004).

99. Notorious B.I.G. featuring R. Kelly, "Fuck You Tonight," *Life After Death*, lyrics available at Original Hip-Hop (Rap) Lyrics Archive, http://www.ohhla.com/anonymous/ntr_big/l_aftr_d/fuck_you.big.txt (accessed March 7, 2004).

100. Snoop Dogg, "Gin and Juice," *Doggystyle* (Death Row Records, 1993), lyrics available at Original Hip-Hop (Rap) Lyrics Archive, http://www.ohhla.com/anonymous/snoopdog/dogstyle/ginjuice.snp.txt (accessed March 5, 2004).

101. Michael Eric Dyson, *Holler If You Hear Me: Searching for Tupac Shakur* (New York: Basic Civitas Books, 2001), 239.

102. Public Enemy, "1 Million Bottlebags," *Apocalypse 91 . . . The Enemy Strikes Back* (Def Jam Records, 1991), lyrics available at Original Hip-Hop (Rap) Lyrics Archive, http://www.ohhla.com/anonymous/pb_enemy/apoc_91/1mil_bag.pbe.txt (accessed March 5, 2004).

103. 2Pac, "Part Time Mutha," *2Pacalyspe Now* (Jive Records, 1992), lyrics available at Original Hip-Hop (Rap) Lyrics Archive, http://www.ohhla.com/anonymous/2_pac/2pclypse/parttime.2pc.txt (accessed March 5, 2004).

104. 2Pac, "Dear Mama," *Me Against the Word* (Jive Records, 1995), lyrics available at Original Hip-Hop (Rap) Lyrics Archive, http://www.ohhla.com/anonymous/2_pac/matworld/dearmama.2pc.txt (accessed March 5, 2004).

105. Ice Cube, "Us," *Death Certificate* (Priority Records, 1991), lyrics available at Original Hip-Hop (Rap) Lyrics Archive, http://www.ohhla.com/anony mous/ice_cube/death/us.cub.txt (accessed March 5, 2004).

106. Ibid.

107. Notorious B.I.G., "Juicy," *Life After Death*, lyrics available at Original Hip-Hop (Rap) Lyrics Archive, http://www.ohhla.com/anonymous/ntr_big/ready_to/juicy.big.txt (accessed March 5, 2004).

108. Kanye West, "We Don't Care," *College Dropout* (Roc-A-Fella Records, 2004), lyrics available at A-Z Lyrics Universe, http://www.azlyrics.com/lyrics/kanyewest/wedontcare.html (accessed March 5, 2003).

109. See Sampsell-Jones, "Culture and Contempt."

110. This is an example of hip-hop's mixed theory of punishment at work. The culture's retributive instinct argues for punishment of drug offenders who harm others—for instance, cocaine sellers. The utilitarian limitations on punishment, however, including the number of minority men who would be incarcerated under an exclusively harm-based regime, militates against punishment.

111. Lawrence M. Friedman, *Crime and Punishment in American History* (New York: Basic Books, 1993), 80 (quoting Charles Dickens, *American Notes* (New York: Penguin, 1972) 146.

112. See Mauer, *Race to Incarcerate*, 12, 23, figs. 2–3.

113. DMX, Method Man, Nas, and Ja Rule, "Grand Finale," *Belly Soundtrack* (Def Jam Records, 1998), lyrics available at Original Hip-Hop (Rap) Lyrics Archive, http://www.ohhla.com/anonymous/misc/hip-hop/grfinale.bly.txt (accessed March 4, 2004).

114. Kelley, "Kickin' Reality," 118.

115. Dead Prez, "Behind Enemy Lines," *Let's Get Free* (Loud Records, 2000), lyrics available at Hip Hop Database, http://www.hhdb.com/lyrics/3184/Behind-Enemy-Lines-Lyrics.

116. Immortal Technique, "Revolutionary," *Revolutionary Volume 1*, lyrics available at Original Hip-Hop (Rap) Lyrics Archive, http://www.ohhla.com/anonymous/immortal/rev_vol1/revolut.tch.txt (accessed February 28, 2004).

117. DMX, "Who We Be," *The Great Depression* (Universal Records, 2001), lyrics available at Original Hip-Hop (Rap) Lyrics Archive, http://www.ohhla.com/anonymous/dmx/thegreat/whowebe.dmx.txt (accessed March 5, 2004).

118. Gang Starr, "Conspiracy," *Daily Operation* (Chrysalis/ERI, 1992), lyrics available at Original Hip-Hop (Rap) Lyrics Archive, http://www.ohhla.com/anonymous/gngstarr/daily_op/conspire.gsr.txt (accessed March 28, 2004).

119. Mos Def, "Mathematics," *Black on Both Sides* (Rawkus Records, 1999), lyrics available at MusicSongLyrics.com, http://www.musicsonglyrics.com/M/mosdeflyrics/mosdefmathematicslyrics.htm.

120. Ras Kass, "Ordo Abchao (Order Out of Chaos)," *Soul on Ice* (Priority Records, 1996), lyrics available at Original Hip-Hop (Rap) Lyrics Archive, http://www.ohhla.com/anonymous/ras_kass/sl_onice/abchao.rsk.txt (accessed March 5, 2004).

121. For an analysis of black women rappers and sexual politics in rap music, see Tricia Rose, *Black Noise: Rap Music and Black Culture in Contemporary America* (Middletown, CT: Wesleyan University Press, 1994), 146–82.

8. Droppin' Science: High-Tech Justice

1. Darren Gowen, "Overview of the Federal Home Confinement Program, 1988–1996," 64-DEC Fed. Probation (2000): 11.

2. Ralph K. Schwitzgebel, "Development and Legal Regulation of Coercive Behavior Modification Techniques with Offenders," National Institute of Mental Health, Bethesda, MD (1977): 15.

3. Thomas G. Toombs, "Monitoring and Controlling Criminal Offenders Using Satellite Global Positioning System Coupled with Surgically Implanted Transponders," *Criminal Justice Policy Review* 7 (1995): 341, 344.

4. Relevant statutes include 18 U.S.C. § 3142(c)(1), which governs restrictions and curfews as a condition for pretrial release, 18 U.S.C. § 3563(b)(19), which authorizes home confinement as a condition for probation or supervised release, and 18 U.S.C. § 3624(c), which allows the final part of a prisoner's term to be served "under conditions that will afford the prisoner a reasonable opportunity to adjust to and prepare for his reentry into the community." Gowen, "Overview of the Federal Home Confinement Program," 11.

5. Ibid., 11–12.

6. Craig Russell, *Alternatives to Prison: Rehabilitation and Other Programs*, (Broomall, PA: Mason Crest Publishers, 2007), 95.

7. Rita Haverkamp et al., "Electronic Monitoring in Europe," *European Journal of Crime, Criminal Law and Criminal Justice* 12 (2004): 36.

8. "If a microchip implant had tracking capabilities, it would be superior to the currently available electronic tether because it would not require the telephone as an adjunct." Elaine M. Ramesh, "Time Enough? Consequences of Human Microchip Implantation," *Risk: Health Safety and Environment* 8 (1997): 373, 385.

9. Maryland has a program that allows offenders who participate in various noncustodial programs to sign in using their thumbprint and a password. If an offender fails to report as scheduled, the kiosk automatically notifies the probation or parole police. Russell, *Alternatives to Prison*, 102.

10. Dorothy K. Kagehiro, "Psycholegal Issues of Home Confinement," *St. Louis University Law Journal* 37 (1993): 647, 656.

11. Todd Lewan, "Chip Implants Linked to Animal Tumors," *Washington Post*, September 8, 2007.

12. Jeneen Interlandi, "What Addicts Need," *Newsweek*, March 3, 2008.

13. Ibid.

14. Chapter 4's proposal for strategic nullification applies only to drug crimes, not to other crimes, like theft, that may be committed by some addicts.

15. Benoit Denizet-Lewis, "An Anti-Addiction Pill," *New York Times*, June 25, 2006.

16. Ovation Pharmaceuticals, "FDA Accepts for Review Ovation's Two NDA Submissions for Sabril," press release, February 27, 2008.

17. Interlandi, "What Addicts Need."

18. Paige Bowers, "How to Put a Police Dog on a Chip," Time.com, January 4, 2004, http://www.time.com/time/magazine/article/0,9171,1101040112-570268,00.html.

19. Thomson Reuters Foundation, Alert Net, http://www.alertnet.org/print able.htm?URL=/thenews/newsdesk/N21180333.htm; http://www.theage.com.au /articles/2004/04/22/1082530272821.html?from=storyrhs.

20. Science GNASA http://science.nasa.gov/headlines/y2004/06oct_enose .htm.

21. "Brain Scanner Is a Lie Detector," BBC Online, November 30, 2004, http://news.bbc.co.uk/2/hi/health/4051211.stm.

22. Richard Willing, "MRI Tests Offer Glimpse at Brains Behind the Lies," USA Today, June 26, 2006, http://www.usatoday.com/tech/science/2006-06-26 -mri-lie_x.htm.

23. Jeff Wise, "Thought Police: How Brain Scans Could Invade Your Private Life," Popular Mechanics, November 2007, available at www.popularmechanics .com/science/research/4226614.html.

24. "Brain Scanner Is a Lie Detector."

25. Willing, "MRI Tests Offer Glimpse."

26. Margaret Talbot, "Duped," New Yorker, July 7, 2002.

27. Michael Peroski, "They (Might) Know What You're Thinking," Science Progress, April 24, 2008, http://www.scienceprogress.org/2008/04/they-might-know-what-youre-thinking/.

28. Sean Kevin Thompson, "The Legality of the Use of Psychiatric Neuroimaging in Intelligence Interrogation," Cornell Law Review 90 (2005): 1601.

29. Ibid., 1605.

30. Faye Flam, "Your Brain May Soon Be Used Against You," Philadelphia Inquirer, October 29, 2002.

31. Steven I. Friedland, "The Criminal Law Implications of the Human Genome Project: Reimagining a Genetically Oriented Criminal Justice System," Kentucky Law Journal 86 (1998): 303, 314.

32. Angela Liang, "Gene Therapy: Legal and Ethical Issues for Pregnant Women," Cleveland State Law Review 47 (1999): 61, 64.

33. Ibid., 64; Michael J. Reiss, "What Sort of People Do We Want? The Ethics of Changing People Through Genetic Engineering," Notre Dame Journal of Law, Ethics and Public Policy 13 (1999): 63, 64 (discussing the three forms of gene therapy).

34. Ibid., 64.

35. Ibid.

36. See ibid.; also Friedland, "Criminal Law Implications," 314, 330–31.

37. Benedict Carey, "Living on the Impulse," New York Times, April 4, 2006, F1.

38. See Friedland, "Criminal Law Implications," 330.

39. Ibid. (referencing the well-known Brunner study of a Dutch family in the 1990s); see also Brent Garland and Mark S. Frankel, "Considering Convergence: A Policy Dialogue about Behavioral Genetics, Neuroscience, and Law; The Impact of Behavioral Genetics on the Criminal Law," Law and Contemporary Problems, January 1, 2006, 103.

40. Laura A. Baker, Serena Bezdjian, and Adrian Raine, "The Impact of Behavioral Genetics on the Criminal Law: Behavioral Genetics: The Sci-

ence of Antisocial Behavior," *Law and Contemporary Problems* 69 (2006): 7, 37.

41. Caspi Avshalom et al., "Role of Genotype in the Cycle of Violence of Mistreated Children," *Science* 297 (2002): 851.

42. See Friedland, "Criminal Law Implications," 335.

43. See Liang, "Gene Therapy," 64.

9. The Beautiful Struggle: Seven Ways to Take Back Justice

1. Peter W. Greenwood, "Diverting Children from a Life of Crime: Measuring Costs and Benefits," RAND, 1996.

2. Ibid.

3. National Center for Education Statistics, http://nces.ed.gov/fastfacts/display .asp?id=27.

4. "School or the Streets: Crime and California's Dropout Crisis," Fight Crime: Invest in Kids California, December 2007, http://www.fightcrime.org/ ca/dropout/CA_Dropout_Report.pdf.

5. Ibid.

6. Ibid., 4.

7. National Council of Juvenile and Family Court Judges, "Blueprints Program: Quantum Opportunities Program," 2005, http://www.ncjfcj.org/content/ blogcategory/242/234/. Other aspects included "youth with case management and mentoring, supplemental after-school education, developmental activities, community service activities, comprehensive supportive services."

8. Ibid.

9. Ibid.

10. "Guide to Effective Programs for Children and Youth: Quantum Opportunities Program." ChildTrends, January 29, 2002, http://www.childtrends.org/ Lifecourse/programs/QuantumOpportunitiesProgram.htm.

11. "Blueprints Model Programs: Quantum Opportunities Program," Center for the Study and Prevention of Violence, http://www.colorado.edu/cspv/blue prints/model/programs/details/QOPdetails.html.

12. "Fulton to Pay Students in After-School Program," *Atlanta Journal-Constitution*, January 22, 2008, http://www.freerepublic.com/focus/f-news/1957 793/posts.

13. Aricka Flowers, "Baltimore Is Paying High School Students to Study," *School Reform News*, Heartland Institute, April 1, 2008, http://www.heart land.org/Article.cfm?artId=22966.

14. Legislative Counsel, State of California, Official California Legislative Information, http://leginfo.ca.gov/cgi-bin/postquery?bill_number=ab_832&sess= 9900&house=B&author=keeley.

15. Sara B. Miller, "How to Keep Those Kids in Class? Pay Them," *Christian Science Monitor*, July 29, 2005.

16. Pamela A. Meyer et al., "Surveillance for Elevated Lead Levels Among Children: United States, 1997–2001," Centers for Disease Control and Preven-

tion, September 2003, available at http://www.cdc.gov/mmwr/preview/mmwr html/ss5210a1.htm.

17. "Lead," National Institute for Occupational Safety and Health, available at http://www.cdc.gov/niosh/topics/lead/.

18. Shankar Vedantam, "Research Links Lead Exposure, Criminal Activity," *Washington Post*, July 8, 2007.

19. Jessica Wolpaw Reyes, "Environmental Policy as Social Policy? The Impact of Childhood Lead Exposure on Crime," Working Paper 13097, May 2007, National Bureau of Economic Research.

20. Vedantam, "Research Links Lead Exposure."

21. Ibid.

22. Roger Masters, "Toxins, Brain Chemistry, and Behavior," http://www.dart mouth.edu/~rmasters/tbcba.htm.

23. Peter B. Lord, "Compromise on Lead Paint Bills," *Providence Journal*, June 7, 2001.

24. "High Point Police Department Wins Innovation Award for Drug Market Strategy Designed by Professor David Kennedy," John Jay College of Criminal Justice, http://www.jjay.cuny.edu/948.php.

25. James M. Frabutt et al., "High Point West End Initiative: Project Description, Log, and Preliminary Impact Analysis," Project Safe Neighborhoods, Center for Youth, Family, and Community Partnerships, University of North Carolina at Greensboro, July 2004, http://www.uncg.edu/csr/pdfs/west%20end%20report .pdf.

26. Ibid.

27. Department of Justice, "Drug Market Intervention Initiative," http://www .ojp.usdoj.gov/BJA/topics/DMII.pdf.

28. For a more complete description, see Paul Butler, "Walking While Black: Encounters with the Police on My Street," *Legal Times*, November 10, 1997.

29. Stuart Taylor Jr., "The Skies Won't Be Safe Until We Use Commonsense Profiling," *National Journal*, March 16, 2002.

30. James Austin et al., "Unlocking America: Why and How to Reduce America's Prison Population," JFA Institute, November 2007, http://www.jfa -associates.com/publications/srs/UnlockingAmerica.pdf. Statistics from David P. Farrington, Patrick A. Langan, and Michael Tonry, eds., *Cross-National Studies in Crime and Justice* (Washington, DC: U.S. Department of Justice, Bureau of Justice Statistics, 2004), and Franklin E. Zimring and Gordon Hawkins, *Crime Is Not the Problem: Lethal Violence in America* (New York: Oxford University Press, 1997).

31. Austin et al., "Unlocking America."

32. Ibid.

33. Kevin Fagan, "Schwarzenegger Studies Early Release of 22,000 Inmates," *San Francisco Chronicle*, December 21, 2007, A1.

34. Michael Rothfeld, "Deal on Prisons Is Possible," *Los Angeles Times*, January 19, 2008, B1.

35. See John Wildermuth, "Prisons: 22,000 Nonviolent Inmates Could Be

Set Free Early," *San Francisco Chronicle*, January 12, 2008, A8; Fagan, "Schwarzenegger Studies Early Release."

36. Fagan, "Schwarzenegger Studies Early Release."

37. Wildermuth, "Prisons."

38. Austin et al., "Unlocking America."

39. Andrew Morton, "Oops, Obama Was for Decriminalizing Marijuana Before He Opposed It," *Los Angeles Times*, February 5, 2008.

40. Kurt Schmoke, "Obama Not Completely Silent on the Drug War," Huffington Post, May 22, 2008, http://www.huffingtonpost.com/kurt-schmoke/obama -not-completely-sile_b_103122.html.

41. Jennifer Haberkorn, "Obama Flip-Flops on Pot," *Washington Times*, January 31, 2008.

42. Ibid.

43. Ibid.

44. Jann S. Wenner, "Bill Clinton Interview with Rolling Stone," *Rolling Stone*, October 6, 2000.

45. John P. MacKenzie, "Editorial Notebook: The Real Clarence Thomas," *New York Times*, June 28, 1993.